PAUL SELIGSON
CAROL LETHABY
TOM ABRAHAM
CRIS GONTOW

Level
1

English ID

Student's Book
& Workbook
Combo Edition
1A

ID SB Language map

	Question syllabus	Vocabulary	Grammar	Speaking & Skills
1				
1.1	Are you Canadian?	Countries & nationalities Adjectives and *a / an* + noun	Verb *be* – ⊕ ⊖ Yes / No ❓ Subject pronouns	Introduce yourself & greetings Ask & answer about countries & nationalities Give opinions about people and places
1.2	How do you spell your last name?	The alphabet Numbers 11–100		Spell words & your name Say your age & where you're from
1.3	What's your email address?	Personal objects / plurals	Verb *be* – Wh- ❓ Demonstrative pronouns	Ask for & give personal information Ask about & identify objects
1.4	Are these your glasses?	Adjectives & colors	Possessive adjectives	Talk about possessions Describe objects
1.5	What's your full name?			Complete a form
	How are you?	Greetings & responses		Meeting people & social interaction
	Writing 1: A social media profile	**ID Café 1:** Role-play a class reunion		
2				
2.1	When do you get up?	Activities & days of the week Time expressions	*go* activities	Describe routine Ask & answer about routine Ask & answer about sleeping habits
2.2	What do you do in the mornings?	Morning routine	Simple present ⊕ ⊖ Prepositions of time	Talk about & compare morning routines
2.3	Who do you live with?	Family	Simple present ❓	Describe family Question intonation Ask and answer simple present questions
2.4	When do you check your phone?	Cell phone expressions	Frequency adverbs	Talk about cell phone habits Do a survey about phone use
2.5	How old are you?			Role-play an interview
	How do you celebrate your birthday?	Special occasions		Use celebratory expressions
	Writing 2: A personal email	**ID Café 2:** Talk about reviews and reports		**Review 1** *p.30*
3				
3.1	What's the weather like?	Weather	*It's* + adjective	Describe weather Ask & answer about weather
3.2	Are you busy at the moment?	Everyday actions (1) Months & seasons	Present continuous ⊕ ⊖	Talk about what's happening now Talk about months & seasons
3.3	What are you doing these days?	Technology problems	Present continuous ❓	Ask & answer about what's happening now Discuss technology problems
3.4	What do you do after school / work?	Everyday actions (2) Verbs for emotion, senses or mental states Future time expressions	Simple present vs. present continuous	Talk about what people are doing now and what they usually do Talk about celebrity activists
3.5	Why are you learning English?		*need to / have to*	Analyze your English
	Are you thirsty?	Adjectives (feelings)	Informal English	Make offers
	Writing 3: A language profile	**ID Café 3:** Discuss photography		
4				
4.1	Do you like tennis?	Sports	Definite article *the*	Talk about sports Pronunciation of *the*
4.2	Can you drive a tractor?	Abilities	*Can*: Yes / No ❓ / short answers	Ask and answer about ability Rank items that can change the world
4.3	What languages can you speak?	Talents	*Can*: ⊕ ⊖ and Wh- ❓ Adverbs	Ask and answer about ability & talents Role-play a job interview
4.4	Are you an organized person?	Clothes	Possessive pronouns Possessive *s*	Talk about what people are wearing Talk about ownership Talk about being messy / tidy
4.5	Do you like spas?	Spa facilities		Read for details Describe a perfect spa day
	What shoe size are you?	Shopping expressions	Punctuation	Shop for clothes
	Writing 4: A job application	**ID Café 4:** Design and present a superhero		**Review 2** *p.56*
5				
5.1	Is there a mall in your area?	Public places	There is / there are ⊕ ⊖ ❓	Describe a town / neighborhood
5.2	What are your likes and dislikes?	Free-time activities Household chores	*like / love / hate / enjoy / not mind* + verb + *-ing*	Talk about likes and dislikes Sentence stress
5.3	What do you like doing on vacation?	Vacation	Comparative adjectives	Talk about vacations and vacation activities Describe a perfect vacation
5.4	How often do you leave voice messages?	House sitting	Object pronouns Imperatives Comparatives / superlatives	Talk about house sitting Give instructions
5.5	What's a staycation?			Give and understand instructions
	Do you live near here?	Giving directions		Give and follow directions
	Writing 5: A city brochure	**ID Café 5:** Talk about personal technology		**Mid-term review** *p.70*

Grammar p. 138   Sounds and usual spelling p. 158   Audioscript p. 160

ID WB Language map

	Question syllabus	Vocabulary	Grammar	Speaking & Skills
1 1.1	Are you Canadian?	Countries & nationalities Adjectives (opinion)	Verb *be* (Present)	Give opinions
1.2	How do you spell your last name?	Numbers 1–10		Introduce yourself
1.3	What's your email address?	Personal objects (singular & plural)	Demonstrative pronouns	
1.4	Are these your glasses?	Adjectives & colors	Possessive adjectives	
1.5	What's your full name?	Greetings		Give personal information
2 2.1	When do you get up?	Days of the week Time *go to* (a / the / –)		Talk about routine
2.2	What do you do in the mornings?	Morning routine	Simple present ⊕ ⊖	Describe your morning routine
2.3	Who do you live with?	Family	Simple present *Wh-* ❓	Answer personal information questions
2.4	When do you check your phone?	Frequency adverbs Cell phone verbs		Talk about how often you do things
2.5	How do you celebrate your birthday?	Special occasions	Frequency adverbs	Process personal information
3 3.1	What's the weather like?	Weather	*It's raining* vs. *It's rainy*	Talk about the weather
3.2	Are you busy at the moment?	Phone phrases	Present continuous	
3.3	What are you doing these days?	Daily actions Technology problems	Present continuous	
3.4	What do you do after school / work?		Simple present vs. Present continuous	Talk about your family
3.5	Why are you learning English?	Adjectives (feelings)	*have to*, *want to*	
4 4.1	Do you like tennis?	Sports		Talk about sports
4.2	Can you drive a tractor?	Abilities	*Can* ⊕ ⊖	Talk about abilities
4.3	What languages can you speak?		*Can* ⊕ ⊖ ❓	Talk about abilities
4.4	Are you an organized person?	Clothes & accessories	Possessive pronouns, Possessive *'s*, & *Whose*	Talk about clothes
4.5	What shoe size are you?	Shopping expressions		
5 5.1	Is there a mall in your area?	Public places	*There is / there are* (Present) ⊕ ⊖ ❓	Describe a town
5.2	What are your likes and dislikes?	Household chores Free-time activities	*like / love / hate / enjoy / not mind* + verb + *-ing*	Talk about likes & dislikes
5.3	What do you like doing on vacation?	Vacation		Talk about vacation activities
5.4	How often do you leave voice messages?	Instructions	Imperatives	
5.5	Do you live near here?	Adjectives		Give directions

Audio script p. 54　　Answer key p. 60　　Phrasebank p. 64　　Wordlist p. 70

English ID

Welcome to English ID!

Finally, an English course you can understand!

Famous **song lines** illustrate language from lessons.

Lesson titles are questions to help you engage with the content.

Word stress in pink on new words.

Contextualized Picture Dictionary to present and review vocabulary.

Focus on **Common mistakes** accelerates accuracy.

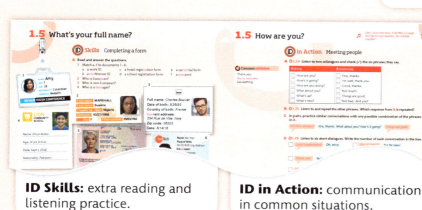

ID Skills: extra reading and listening practice.

ID in Action: communication in common situations.

Authentic videos present topics in real contexts.

ID Café: sitcom videos to consolidate language.

Reviews systematically recycle language.

A complete **Grammar** reference with exercises.

Welcome

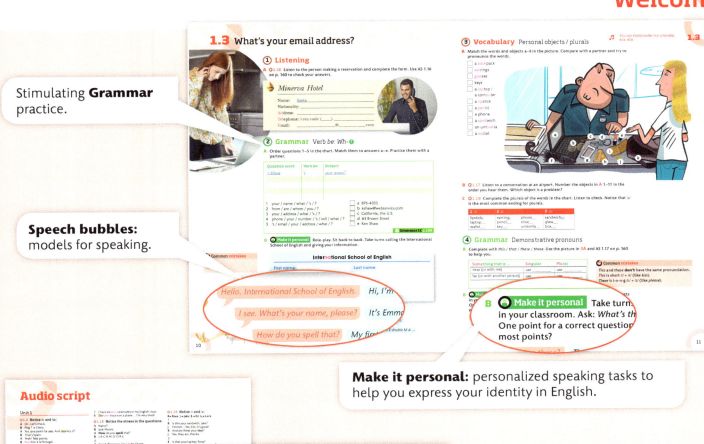

Stimulating **Grammar** practice.

Speech bubbles: models for speaking.

Make it personal: personalized speaking tasks to help you express your identity in English.

Audio script activities to consolidate pronunciation.

Pictures to present and practice **Pronunciation**.

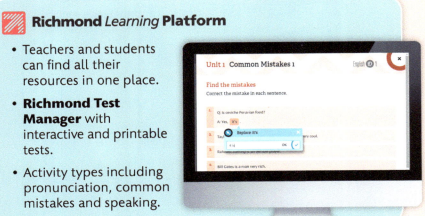

Richmond *Learning* **Platform**

- Teachers and students can find all their resources in one place.
- **Richmond Test Manager** with interactive and printable tests.
- Activity types including pronunciation, common mistakes and speaking.

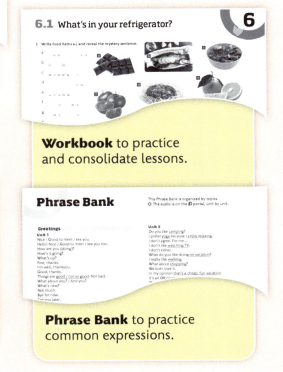

Workbook to practice and consolidate lessons.

Phrase Bank to practice common expressions.

Learn to express your identity in English!

1.1 Are you Canadian?

1 Vocabulary Countries and nationalities

A ▶1.1 Listen and (circle) the correct words. Introduce yourself to the class.

Hello / Hi! My name's *Marty / Judy* and I'm *Brazilian / Mexican / American.*
I'm from *New York / Mexico City / Brasilia.* Nice / Good to see / meet you.

B ▶1.2 Match flags 1–8 to the countries. Listen to the quiz to check. What's your score?

- [ ] The U.S.
- [ ] China
- [ ] Argentina
- [ ] Canada
- [ ] The UK
- [ ] Portugal
- [ ] Peru
- [ ] Spain

C ▶1.3 Match the nationalities to countries 1–8 in **B**. Guess the pronunciation. Listen to check. Notice the **unstressed suffixes**.

- [ ] Peruvian
- [ ] Spanish
- [ ] American
- [ ] Chinese
- [ ] Argentinian
- [ ] British
- [ ] Canadian
- [ ] Portuguese

D 👤 **Make it personal** Say the names of countries and nationalities near your country.

Bolivia – Bolivian

2 Grammar Verb *be* ➕➖ and *Yes / No* ❓

🎵 When I see your face, There's not a thing that I would change, 'Cause you're amazing, Just the way you are.

1.1

A ▶1.4 Listen to the questions and answers. Complete the grammar box. Use contractions where possible. Listen again to check.

➕	❓	➕➖ Short answers
I'm Chinese.	<u>Am</u> I Chinese?	Yes, you *are*. / No, you're not.
You're Argentinian.	_____ you Argentinian?	No, I _____. / Yes, I _____.
She's Brazilian.	_____ she Brazilian?	No, she _____. / Yes, she _____.
He's Colombian.	_____ he Colombian?	No, he _____. / Yes, he _____.
It's Indian.	_____ it Indian?	No, it _____. / Yes, it _____.
We're Chilean.	<u>Are</u> we Chilean?	Yes, we *are*. / No, we *aren't*.
They're Ecuadorian.	<u>Are</u> they Ecuadorian?	Yes, they *are*. / No, they *aren't*.

➡ Grammar 1A p. 138

✋ Common mistakes

Are you
~~You are~~ Latin American?
   we are.
Yes, ~~we're~~.
     Chinese
Are you ~~chineses~~?

B 🟢 Make it personal ▶1.5 Listen to the example dialogue. Look at the photos on p. 6. In pairs, ask and answer about the people, countries, and nationalities to identify the photos.

> Photo 5 … Shawn Mendes and Drake. Are they American?   No, they aren't. They're Canadian.

C ▶1.6 Listen to check. Did you identify all of the photos correctly?

3 Vocabulary Adjectives and *a / an* + noun

A ▶1.7 Listen and put the positive and negative adjectives in the right place.

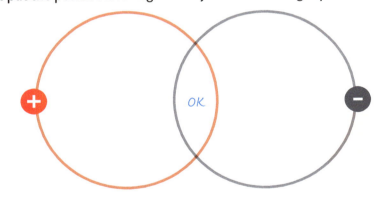

amazing
cool
excellent
fantastic
horrible
important
intelligent
interesting
~~OK~~
rich
ridiculous
terrible

✋ Common mistakes

He's an interesting person.
He's ~~a person interesting~~.
It's a very cool city.
It's ~~a city very cool~~.

B ▶1.8 Listen to the opinions about people and places. Complete 1–8 with *a / an*.

1 He's _____ amazing player.
2 It's _____ cool monument.
3 She's _____ rich person.
4 She's _____ intelligent person.
5 It's _____ horrible city.
6 It's _____ interesting country.
7 He's _____ excellent teacher.
8 She's _____ fantastic actor.

C Complete the rules with the correct word.

   a   nouns   adjectives   an

1 Use _____ before a consonant sound.
2 Use _____ before a vowel sound.
3 In English, _____ come before _____.

D 🟢 Make it personal Think of five different countries and a famous person / place in each one. In pairs, give your opinions about them.

> Chichén Itzá is a Mayan city in Mexico. It's an amazing place!   Yes, I agree.

> Lady Gaga is an American musician. I think she's ridiculous!   I disagree. She's amazing!

1.2 How do you spell your last name?

1 Pronunciation The alphabet

A ▶1.9 Match the pairs of words to the pictures in **B**. Listen, check, and repeat.

- [ ] a shoe • two
- [ ] a car • a star
- [ ] a pen • ten
- [ ] a nose • a rose
- [1] a plane • a train
- [ ] three • a tree
- [ ] nine • wine

B ▶1.10 Listen to the words and letters in the chart and notice the vowel sounds.

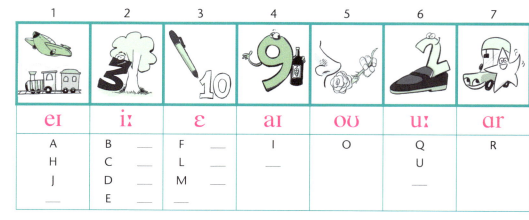

1	2	3	4	5	6	7
eɪ	iː	ɛ	aɪ	oʊ	uː	ɑr
A	B ___	F ___	I	O	Q	R
H	C ___	L ___			U	
J	D ___	M ___			___	
___	E					

C ▶1.11 Listen to these letters and put them in the correct column in **B**.

G   K   N   P   S   T   V   W   X   Y   Z

> ⓘ **Common mistakes**
> How do you spell that?
> ~~How can I write?~~

D 🧑 **Make it personal** Point to a picture. Ask your partner to say it. Which vowel sound is it? Try to spell the word. Use a dictionary if necessary.

What's that?   *It's rain.*   *How do you spell "rain"?*   *R-A-I-N*   *Correct!*

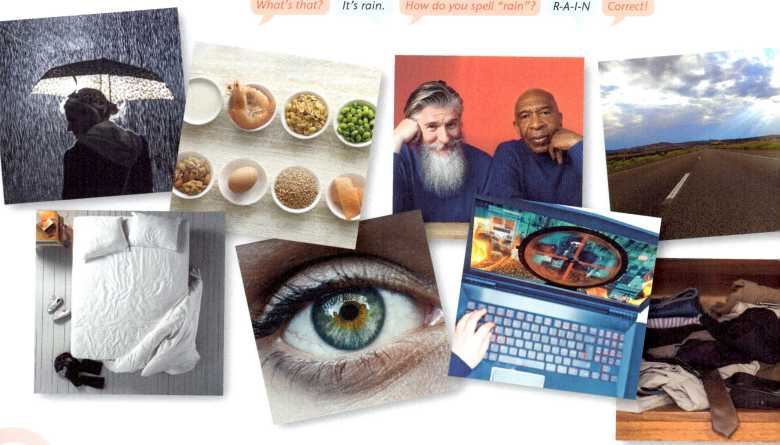

8

2 Vocabulary Numbers 11–100

♪ *It's fun to stay at the Y.M.C.A.*   1.2

A ▶ 1.12 Complete the numbers under the prices. Listen, check, and repeat with the correct stress.

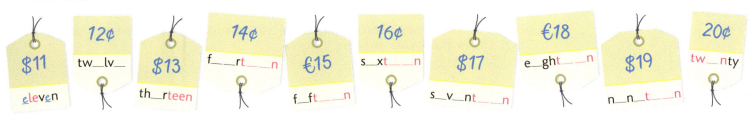

$11 — eleven
12¢ — tw_lv_
$13 — th_rteen
14¢ — f___rt___n
€15 — f_ft___n
16¢ — s_xt___n
$17 — s_v_nt___n
€18 — e_ght___n
$19 — n_n_t___n
20¢ — tw_nty

B ▶ 1.13 How do you say these numbers? Listen, check, and repeat with the correct stress.

30 40 50 60 70 80 90 100   *Thirty, forty ...*

C ▶ 1.14 Listen to sentences 1–8 and circle the number you hear.

1 18 80 85   3 20 11 12   5 15 50 55   7 06 60 16
2 17 70 73   4 19 90 99   6 14 40 43   8 13 30 33

D 👤 **Make it personal** Play *Bingo*. Write numbers from 1 to 20 on the card.

One student: Call numbers from 1 to 20 in any order.
Winner: Shout *Bingo!* when you complete a line.

Play again with numbers from 21 to 40, 41 to 60, etc.

3 Listening

A ▶ 1.15 Listen to five dialogues and circle the names you hear. Use AS 1.15 on p. 160 to check your answers.

1 **First name:** Jack / Jake   **Last name:** Noore / Moore
2 **Full name:** Peter / Dieter   Queen / Quinn
3 **Name:** Rochelle / Roxalle   Johns / Jones
4 **First name:** George / Jeorge   **Last name:** Wessex / Essex
5 **Full name:** Joy / Joi   Boscombi / Boscombe

🚫 **Common mistakes**
I'm 18 (years old).
~~I have 18 years.~~

B 👤 **Make it personal** In pairs, practice the dialogues with your own name and names of people you know. Say your age, too.

What's your name, please? Bruce Wayne. *How do you spell that?* B-R-U-C-E W-A-Y-N-E. I'm 18.

Are you British? No, I'm from Gotham City.

1.3 What's your email address?

1 Listening

A ▶ 1.16 Listen to the person making a reservation and complete the form. Use AS 1.16 on p. 160 to check your answers.

Minerva Hotel

Name: Karin
Nationality: _____
Address: _____
Telephone: Area code (____) _____
Email: _____@_____.com

2 Grammar Verb *be*: Wh- ❓

A Order questions 1–5 in the chart. Match them to answers a–e. Practice them with a partner.

Question word	Verb *be*	Subject
1 What	's	your name?

1 your / name / what / 's / ?
2 from / are / where / you / ?
3 your / address / what / 's / ?
4 phone / your / number / 's / cell / what / ?
5 's / email / your / address / what / ?

☐ a 876-4033
☐ b kshaw@webservice.com
☐ c California, the U.S.
☐ d 85 Brown Street
☐ e Ken Shaw

➡ **Grammar 1C** p. 138

B 🗣 **Make it personal** Role-play. Sit back to back. Take turns calling the International School of English and giving your information.

🔊 **Common mistakes**

I'm ^a student.

International School of English

First name: Last name:
Address:
Phone number:
Email address:

Hello. International School of English. — Hi, I'm a student.
I see. What's your name, please? — It's Emma Miranda.
How do you spell that? — My first name is E-double M-A …

10

🎵 *You can stand under my umbrella, ella, ella.* **1.3**

③ Vocabulary Personal objects / plurals

A Match the words and objects a–k in the picture. Compare with a partner and try to pronounce the words.

- [ ] a backpack
- [ ] earrings
- [ ] glasses
- [ ] keys
- [ ] a laptop / a computer
- [ ] a lipstick
- [ ] a pencil
- [ ] a phone
- [ ] a sandwich
- [ ] an umbrella
- [ ] a wallet

B ▶1.17 Listen to a conversation at an airport. Number the objects in **A** 1–11 in the order you hear them. Which object is a problem?

C ▶1.18 Complete the plurals of the words in the chart. Listen to check. Notice that /z/ is the most common ending for plurals.

1 /s/	2 /z/		3 /ɪz/
lipstick*s*	earring*s*	phone__	sandwich*es*
laptop__	pencil__	shoe__	glass__
wallet__	key__	umbrella__	box__

④ Grammar Demonstrative pronouns

A Complete with *this / that / these / those*. Use the picture in **3A** and AS 1.17 on p. 160 to help you.

Something that is …	Singular	Plural
near (or with me)	use _____	use _____
far (or with another person)	use _____	use _____

➡ **Grammar 1D** p. 138

⚠ **Common mistakes**

This and *these* **don't** have the same pronunciation.
This is short /ɪ/ + /s/ (like *kiss*).
These is l-o-n-g /iː/ + /z/ (like *please*).

B 🔘 **Make it personal** Take turns to test a partner with the picture in **3A** and objects in your classroom. Ask: *What's this? What's that? What are these? What are those?* One point for a correct question and one point for a correct answer. Who scored the most points?

What are these?   *They're windows.*   *What's that?*   *It's a door.*

11

1.4 Are these your glasses?

1 Listening

A ▶1.19 Listen to conversations 1–6 and match them to the pictures.

Is this _____ sandwich, Jake?
Are these _____ keys?

That's _____ laptop!

Are these _____ glasses?

No, they aren't _____ earrings.

I think it's _____ phone.
I think it's _____ phone.

Come on, Ed! These are _____ chips!

Hey! Those are _____ potato chips!

B ▶1.19 Complete the sentences in pictures 1–6 with the correct word. Listen again and use AS 1.19 on p. 160 to check.

her   his   my   our   their   your

2 Grammar Possessive adjectives

A ▶1.19 Match the item from **1A** to the owner. Listen to check.

1 po**ta**to chips   Ed
2 earrings   Lara
3 glasses   Rosa
4 sandwich   Jake
5 phone   Jake and Rosa
6 laptop

B Complete the grammar box.

Subject	Possessive adjective + noun
I	*my* phone
you	_____ keys
_____	her friend
he	_____ shoes
_____	our house
they	_____ **break**fast

→ Grammar 1E p. 138

> **Common mistakes**
> Are these your glasses?
> ~~Is this your glasses?~~

> **Common mistakes**
> *her*
> Lisa's online with ~~your~~ boyfriend.
> *his*
> John loves ~~your~~ girlfriend.

C 🎤 **Make it personal** In groups, each person puts one item in a bag. Take the items out in turn. Point and say what the things are using different possessive adjectives.

This is your pen.   This is his phone.   These are her keys.   These are our keys.

12

♪ *Purple rain, purple rain, I only want to see you bathing in the purple rain.*   1.4

3 Vocabulary Adjectives and colors

A ▶1.20 In pairs, take the quiz. Match the answers to questions a–j and photos 1–10. Listen, check, and repeat the colors.

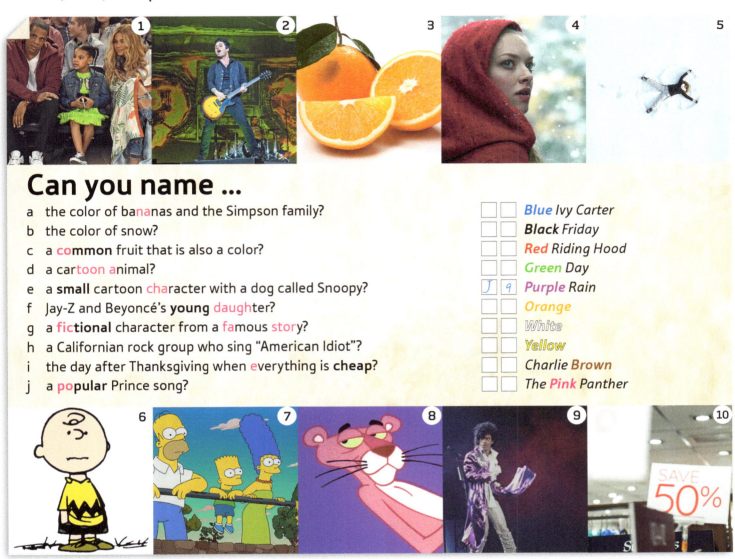

Can you name …

a   the color of ba**na**nas and the Simpson family?
b   the color of snow?
c   a **co**mmon fruit that is also a color?
d   a car**too**n **a**nimal?
e   a **small** cartoon cha**ra**cter with a dog called Snoopy?
f   Jay-Z and Beyoncé's **young** **daugh**ter?
g   a **fic**tional character from a **fa**mous sto**ry**?
h   a Californian rock group who sing "American Idiot"?
i   the day after Thanksgiving when **e**verything is **cheap**?
j   a **po**pular Prince song?

☐ ☐ **Blue** Ivy Carter
☐ ☐ **Black** Friday
☐ ☐ **Red** Riding Hood
☐ ☐ **Green** Day
J   9 **Purple** Rain
☐ ☐ **Orange**
☐ ☐ **White**
☐ ☐ **Yellow**
☐ ☐ Charlie **Brown**
☐ ☐ The **Pink** Panther

B Underline all the adjectives in the quiz. Circle the correct rules.
Adjectives go **before** / **after** the noun.
Adjectives have **a** / **no** plural form.

C Match the **bold** adjectives in the quiz to their opposites. Test your partner.
1   rare _____
2   ex**pen**sive _____
3   big _____
4   real _____
5   unpopular _____
6   old _____

What's the opposite of "rare"?   common

⚠ **Common mistakes**
                        blue eyes
My brother has ~~eyes blues~~.

D ▶1.21 Listen to descriptions of five items in the pictures in **1A** on p. 12. Name them after the beep. Then listen to the answer.

E 👤 **Make it personal** In small groups.
A: Describe an object in the room and give an opinion about it.
B and C: Ask questions and guess what the object is.

They're small and black, and they're really cool!   *Are they my glasses?*   *Yes, they are!*

13

1.5 What's your full name?

🆔 Skills Completing a form

A Read and answer the questions.

1 Match a–f to documents 1–6.
   a a work ID c a hotel registration form e a car rental form
   b a conference ID d a school registration form f a passport
2 Who is European?
3 Who is non-European?
4 Who is a teenager?

1
NAME: Amy
SEX: F
AGE: 18
NATIONALITY: Colombian
ADDRESS: Medellín
DESIGN YOUTH CONFERENCE

2
Last name: MARSHALL
First name: Susana
Country of origin: Nigeria
Birthdate: 10/27/1988
Gender: F
Plate number: 6VBV764

3
Full name: Charles Bouvier
Date of birth: 5/26/90
Country of birth: France
Current address:
354 Rue de Ville, Nice
Zip code: 06200
Date: 8/14/18

4
LION COMMUNITY SCHOOL
Name: Omar Aslam
Age: 14 yrs 8 mos
Date: Sept 1, 2018
Nationality: Pakistani

5
UNITED KINGDOM OF GREAT BRITAIN AND NORTHERN IRELAND
Type P Code GBR No. 70125698
Surname (1) MURPHY
Given name(s) (2) GILLIAN JANE
Nationality (3) BRITISH CITIZEN
Date of Birth (4) FEB 15, 1965
Sex (5) F
P<GBRMURPHY<<GILLIAN<<JANE<<<<<<<<<<<<<<<<<
70125698GBR128963456F1890024<<<<<<<<<<<<<05

6
SunTech
Name: Ken Tran
Place of birth: Ho Chi Minh City, Vietnam
Department: Human Resources
Email address: ktran@suntech.com
Tel: 765-3000 Ext: 145

B Read the documents again and find different ways to refer to:
1 your name (5): *first name*
2 your age (3):
3 where you are from (4):

C ▶1.22 Do you know all the countries and nationalities in the documents in **A**? Listen to check.

D ▶1.23 Listen to and complete the registration form.

Second International Conference
Telephone registration

Name: Nationality:
Address: Telephone:
  Email:
Zip Code:

Common mistakes
full
What's your ~~complete~~ name?
current
My ~~actual~~ address is ...

E 🔴 **Make it personal** Choose a document from this page. Ask your partner questions to complete it with their data. Change roles. Then present your partner to the class.

This is my friend, Adriana. Her full name is ...

1.5 How are you?

Hey, I just met you, And this is crazy, But here's my number, So call me, maybe?

ID in Action Meeting people

A ▶ 1.24 Listen to two colleagues and check (✓) the six phrases they say.

Asking	Answering
☐ How are you?	☐ Fine, thanks.
☐ How's it going?	☐ I'm well, thank you.
☐ How are you doing?	☐ Good, thanks.
☐ What about you?	☐ Not much.
☐ What's up?	☐ Things are good.
☐ What's new?	☐ Not bad. And you?

Common mistakes

Thank you.
You're welcome.
~~For nothing.~~

B ▶ 1.25 Listen to and repeat the other phrases. Which response from **A** is repeated?

C In pairs, practice similar conversations with any possible combination of the phrases in **A**.

> Hi! How are you?   Fine, thanks. What about you? How's it going?   Things are good.

D ▶ 1.26 Listen to six short dialogues. Write the number of each conversation in the box.

☐ I don't understand. — Oh, sorry.   ☐ See you later! — Bye for now!

☐ Thank you! — You're welcome.   ☐ Excuse me. Can you say that again, please? — Sure ...

☐ I'm sorry. — Don't worry about it.   ☐ Excuse me. — Oh, I'm sorry.

E **Make it personal** In pairs, imagine you're the people in photos 1–5. Role-play conversations using appropriate expressions.

Writing 1 A social media profile

Tell me, where are you now that I need ya? Where are you now?

A Read Cristina's personal profile and complete the form.

e-pals.net

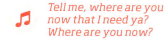

Cristina González

@cristina0330

My name's Cristina González, and I'm 18 years old. I'm Bolivian, from Santa Cruz, but now I live in Toronto, Canada, and I'm a student at Great Lakes High School five days a week. I also work in a local café on weekends. It's popular with students and artists, and the customers are really interesting. Sometimes I don't understand what people say to me, but I'm a fast learner! I don't have a boyfriend at the moment, but I have an amazing best friend called Anya. We go to the gym together. We also go to parties and clubs! Toronto's a fantastic city with an excellent baseball team, the Blue Jays. Anya doesn't like baseball, but I love it. I go alone or with my dad. Please message me: **@cristina0330**.

Profile

Last name:	
First name:	
Age:	
Nationality:	
Country of residence:	
Occupation:	
Username:	

B Read **Write it right!**, then underline the contractions and the connectors in **A**.

Write it right!

In informal writing, use contractions: *I'm, I don't*.
Use a variety of connectors: *and, but, or*.

C Find and correct 10 more mistakes in Luís' reply to Cristina.

Messages

LU_PORT:

Hi, Cristina, my name is Luís, i'm portuguese and I have 19 years. Wow! You live in Toronto – that is excelent. I live in Porto with my mother and father, and I have a lot of parents here. I too study english, but its very dificult! My brother play baseball, maybe you can meet him, ha-ha! Me, I like the soccer. Pleas email me at **luisporto94@e-mates.com** and tell me much about Toronto.

D From the texts in **A** and **C**, which questions can we answer about Cristina (C), Luís (L), or both (B)?

1. Where are you from? ____
2. How old are you? ____
3. What's your full name? ____
4. Where do you live? ____
5. Who do you live with? ____
6. What's your email address? ____
7. Do you go to school? ____
8. Do you have any brothers or sisters? ____
9. Do they play sports? ____
10. Do you have a boyfriend / girlfriend? ____
11. Do you have a best friend? ____
12. What are your interests? ____

E **Make it personal** Write a similar profile of yourself. Write 120–150 words.

Before	Answer questions 1–12 in **D**. Think about extra information, e.g., your opinion about people, places, or things.
While	Use contractions and a variety of connectors. Use adjectives to give your opinion.
After	Check your profile carefully. Show it to a partner before giving it to your teacher.

1 An excellent reunion

1 Before watching

A Complete 1–3 with the correct words.
1 This _____ Andrea. She's at _____ class reunion.
2 This _____ her brother. _____ name is August.
3 That's _____ cousin, Genevieve. She _____ Canadian.

B 🔘 Make it personal What's your opinion of class, work, family, or old friend reunions? Talk in pairs.

> I think class reunions are fun.   Not me. I think they're boring.

2 While watching

A Watch the video and circle the correct answer.
1 The party is **in an apartment** / **at a school**.
2 On the wall are some **new pictures** / **class photos**.
3 **August** / **Andrea** remembers where Kitty is from.
4 **Andrea** / **Genevieve** isn't happy at first.
5 **Andrea** / **Genevieve** says, "I'm so glad you're just my cousin."

B Where are they from? Listen and complete the chart.

Classmate	Country / city	Nationality
Manny Vasquez	_____	Peruvian
_____ Findley	England	_____
_____ Jones	_____	Irish
_____ Belucci	_____	American
_____ Jones	_____	British

C Watch and check (✓) all Genevieve's nicknames you hear.
☐ Gen ☐ Gertrude ☐ Gigi ☐ Jenny ☐ Vie-Vie

D Watch and check (✓) all August's nicknames you hear.
☐ Auggie ☐ Augustus ☐ Gigi ☐ Guto ☐ Iggy

E 🔘 Make it personal Do you have a nickname? What do your family, friends, and classmates usually call you?

> My name's Kathleen, but my friends call me Kathy. What's your nickname?   Please, call me Fred.

3 After watching

A True (T) or False (F)?
1 Mrs. Grandby's an old classmate.
2 With Mrs. Grandby, there's never trouble.
3 Ignatius Dansbury's a great guy.
4 Ignatius is in a class above August and Andrea.
5 Joe Bellucci's a rock star.
6 Johnny's Genevieve's old boyfriend.
7 The cute boys from the band are from Canada.

B In pairs, check your answers to **A**. Correct the false statements.

> I think number 1 is false.   Me, too. I think she's their ...

C Complete and match the greetings to speakers 1–5. There's one extra person.
1 Andrea   ☐ Oh, hey! It's Genevieve.
2 August   ☐ _____, Gen. How are you?
3 Ignatius   ☐ Hey, _____, what's up?
4 Genevieve   ☐ I'm so _____ to see you!
5 Joe   ☐ Iggy! What's up?

D In pairs, take turns saying phrases 1–12 with the correct intonation. Who says them, August (A), Andrea (An), Genevieve (G), or Joe (J)?
1 Guess who's over there? ____
2 Isn't that Manny? ____
3 What a horrible guy! ____
4 Forget about it! ____
5 Really? ____
6 Wait, isn't your middle name something with a G? ____
7 That's not the point. ____
8 Don't you say it! ____
9 Get it? ____
10 Stop it, little Guto! ____
11 Don't worry, ladies. ____
12 Geez! Don't drop it! ____

E 🔘 Make it personal Role-play a class reunion. Imagine you're old friends. In groups of three, gossip!

> Wow, guess who's here? It's Gloria!
>
> No way! Really? Incredible.
>
> That's not Gloria. She's too young. And Gloria's in Mexico.

17

2

2.1 When do you get up?

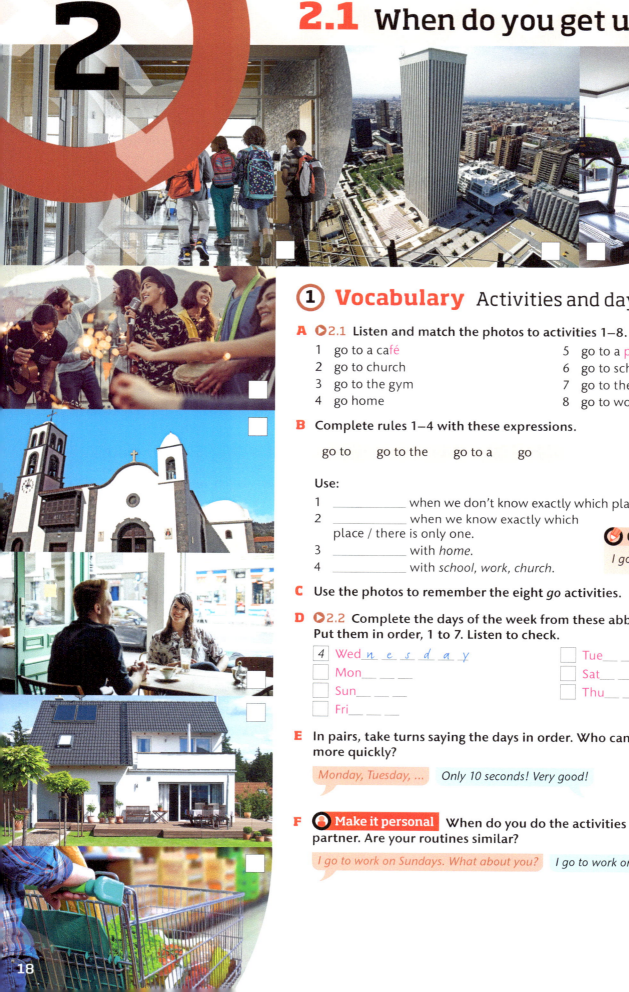

1 Vocabulary Activities and days of the week

A ▶2.1 Listen and match the photos to activities 1–8.
1 go to a café
2 go to church
3 go to the gym
4 go home
5 go to a party
6 go to school
7 go to the grocery store
8 go to work

B Complete rules 1–4 with these expressions.

go to   go to the   go to a   go

Use:
1 _____ when we don't know exactly which place it is.
2 _____ when we know exactly which place / there is only one.
3 _____ with *home*.
4 _____ with *school, work, church*.

> **Common mistakes**
> I go to home at about 8 p.m.

C Use the photos to remember the eight *go* activities.

D ▶2.2 Complete the days of the week from these abbreviations. Put them in order, 1 to 7. Listen to check.

[4] Wed*n_e_s_d_a_y*	[ ] Tue__ __ __ __
[ ] Mon__ __ __	[ ] Sat__ __ __ __
[ ] Sun__ __ __	[ ] Thu__ __ __ __
[ ] Fri__ __ __	

E In pairs, take turns saying the days in order. Who can say them more quickly?

> Monday, Tuesday, …   Only 10 seconds! Very good!

F 🔴 **Make it personal** When do you do the activities in **A**? Compare with a partner. Are your routines similar?

> I go to work on Sundays. What about you?   I go to work on Saturdays.

18

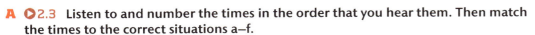
I don't care if Monday's blue. Tuesday's gray and Wednesday too. Thursday I don't care about you.

2.1

② Listening

A ▶2.3 Listen to and number the times in the order that you hear them. Then match the times to the correct situations a–f.

a at a soccer game   c on TV   e at an airport
b at a party   d at school   f at home

B Write more times for your partner to practice saying.

What time is it?   *It's 5:15.*

C ▶2.4 Listen to two short interviews and write the days and times.

1. The woman gets up at _____ in the morning. She goes to school at _____. She goes to bed at _____ during the week. She gets _____ hours of sleep a night.
2. The man goes to work at _____ from _____ to _____. He gets home at _____ in the evening. He doesn't work at night or on weekends.

D ▶2.4 Listen again and complete the rules with *on*, *in*, or *at*.

Use:
1. _____ with times and *night*.
2. _____ with days of the week and *weekends*.
3. _____ with the *morning* / *afternoon* / *evening*.

E 🗣 **Make it personal** In pairs, take turns asking and answering 1–4.
From Monday to Friday, and on weekends, what time do you …
1. get up?
2. go to bed?
3. go to school / work / university?
4. get home from work / school?

I get up at 7 a.m. during the week, but at around 9 on weekends!

I get up early on weekends, around 6:30! I go to work.

⚠ **Common mistakes**

I don't work ~~in~~ *at* the night.

She doesn't go to bed early ~~in~~ *on* weekends.

③ Reading

A Read the report and complete the chart.

On average, how many hours do people in these countries sleep?			
France		Japan	
The U.S.		South Korea	

B 🗣 **Make it personal** Do a class survey. Ask:
1. What time do you get up a) on weekdays b) on weekends?
2. What time do you go to bed a) on weekdays b) on weekends?
3. On average, how many hours do people in your class sleep?

The World Sleeps

The Organization for Economic Cooperation and Development asked 18 countries, "How many hours do you sleep?". The French get an average of 8 hours and 50 minutes of sleep a night compared to the U.S. with 8 hours and 38 minutes. The South Koreans only sleep 7 hours and 49 minutes a night, and the Japanese about 8 hours.

2.2 What do you do in the mornings?

1 Vocabulary Morning routine

A Match pictures a–j with phrases 1–10.

1. ☐ brush my teeth
2. ☐ exercise / work out
3. ☐ get dressed
4. ☐ get up
5. ☐ have breakfast
6. ☐ leave home
7. ☐ make the bed
8. ☐ shave
9. ☐ take a shower
10. ☐ wake up

B ▶ 2.5 Listen to 10 sound effects. Say the phrase before the audio. Were you correct?

C ▶ 2.6 Listen to Jake describe his morning routine. Match the time expressions to his actions in **A**.

☐ 6:30
☐ not immediately
☐ for 30 minutes
☐ 8 a.m.

D 🔴 **Make it personal** Write down your morning routine and the time you do each activity. Compare with a partner. Are your routines similar or different?

I wake up at 6 a.m. You wake up at 7:30 a.m. That's very different!

⚠ **Common mistakes**

What time ̷you get up?
       do

② Grammar Simple present ⊕ and ⊖

♪ *Don't forget me, I beg, I remember you said, Sometimes it lasts in love but sometimes it hurts instead.* 2.2

A Look at the man in the photo. What is his morning routine? Put the activities in **1A** on p. 20 in the order you think the man does them.

B ▶2.7 Listen and check your guesses. Any surprises?

C Study the song line above and Common mistakes. Then read and complete the grammar box.

> **a** Complete the sentences with the ⊕ form of the verb in parentheses.
>
> | | Subject | Verb | |
> |---|---|---|---|
> | 1 | I | | home at 7 a.m. (**leave**) |
> | 2 | You | | to school at 7:30 a.m. (**go**) |
> | 3 | My sister | | her bed in the morning. (**make**) |
> | 4 | My dad | | a shower at night. (**take**) |
> | 5 | My brother and I | | up at 6 a.m. (**get**) |
> | 6 | My friends | | breakfast at 10 a.m. (**have**) |
>
> **b** Complete the rules about ⊖ sentences in the simple present.
>
> I **don't** watch TV when I get home.   She **doesn't** have breakfast.
> 1 We use **does / doesn't** with she / he / it, and we use **doesn't / don't** with all other pronouns.
> 2 **Don't** or **doesn't** goes **before / after** the verb.
>
> **c** Make the sentences in **a** negative.
>
> ➔ **Grammar 2A** p. 140

⊘ Common mistakes

wakes
She / He ~~wake~~ up at 6:00 a.m.
doesn't
She ~~don't~~ wake up before 9:00 a.m.
has
He ~~have~~ breakfast alone.

I wake up at 7 a.m., but I get up at 7:30. I don't make my bed!

D ▶2.7 Complete the paragraph about the man's actions. Then listen to check. Is your morning routine similar?

He <u>wakes up</u> (wake up) at 8 a.m., but he _____ (get up). He sleeps again and then he _____ (get up) at 8:50 a.m., but he _____ (wake up)! After he wakes up, he _____ (make his bed). Then he _____ (exercise) and he _____ (shave). After that, he _____ (take a shower), he _____ (brush his teeth), and he _____ (get dressed)!

E ⊘ **Make it personal** In groups, play the game.
1 Guess and write four ⊕ and ⊖ sentences about the routines and everyday activities of the people in your group.
2 Take turns checking your guesses. Say one of your sentences and ask the other students to raise their hands if the sentence is true for them.

I think three people go to the gym on weekends. Is that true?   *No, it isn't! Only one person goes to the gym on weekends.*

2.3 Who do you live with?

1 Reading and vocabulary Family

A ▶2.8 Who are these characters from an **an**imated TV show? Listen to and read this ad. Then complete their **fa**mily tree.

Meet the Griffins!

Peter Griffin and his wife, Lois, have three **chil**dren. Meg is their first child and their only daughter. Chris is their **teen**age son, and Stewie is his baby brother. He's just one year old. The family is com**ple**ted by Brian, the talking dog, and Peter's **pa**rents, Francis and Thelma. They live in Quahog, Rhode Island, in the U.S.

Watch this show every weeknight at 11:30 p.m. on Channel 44.

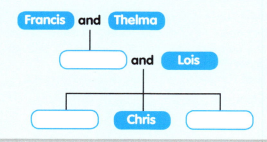

B ▶2.8 Complete the family chart with words from the ad. Then read them aloud to your partner. Listen and check your pronunciation.

Female	Male	Male and female
grandmother	**grand**father	**grand**parent(s)
mother	**fa**ther	_____(s)
sister	_____	**sib**lings / twin(s)
_____	son	child / children
niece	**ne**phew	
_____	**hus**band	couple
aunt	uncle	
		cousin(s)
girlfriend	boyfriend	**part**ner

> **Common mistakes**
> ~~parents~~
> I have two ~~fathers~~: my mom and dad. The others in my family are my ~~parents~~.
> relatives

Lois to Peter? *Lois is his wife.*

C In pairs, test each other on the relationships in **A**.

D Repeat **C**, this time using the possessive 's.   *Who's Francis?* *Thelma's husband.*

E 🔴 **Make it personal** In small groups, draw another famous family tree (from TV, **mo**vies, **li**terature) and write a short ad. Answer questions 1–4.
1 What are their names?
2 Who is who? What are their relationships?
3 Where do they live?
4 What is different or interesting about them?

F Exchange ads with another group. Do you know the family? Who has the best ad?

2 Grammar Simple present

*We are family, I got all my sisters with me,
We are family, Get up everybody and sing!* **2.3**

A Do you know your partner? Guess her / his answers to questions 1–4. Then check.
1 Who does X live with?
 a a friend / relative
 b no one
2 Does X study another language?
 a No, just English.
 b Yes, X studies _____ (language).
3 Which soccer team does X support?
 a _____ (soccer team)
 b X doesn't like soccer / have a team.
4 Does X prefer …
 a tea / coffee?
 b juice / water?

I think you live alone.

No, that's wrong. I live with my parents.

B Complete the grammar box. Are the questions in **A** ASI or QASI?

> There are two different types of questions. Match the word order to each type.
> 1 A question that asks for **information**. *Where does she live?*
> 2 A question to which the **answer** is *Yes* or *No*. *Does he play soccer?*
>
> ☐ **A**uxiliary verb + **s**ubject + **i**nfinitive verb? (ASI)
> ☐ **Q**uestion word + **a**uxiliary verb + **s**ubject + **i**nfinitive verb? (QASI)

➔ **Grammar 2B** p.140

C Are these *Yes / No* (Y / N) or information (I) questions?
1 ☐ What's your full name?
2 ☐ Are you Spanish?
3 ☐ Where do you live?
4 ☐ Do you live with your parents?
5 ☐ Where exactly in the U.S. do you plan to travel to?
6 ☐ Do you know anyone in Alaska?

D ▶ 2.9 Match questions 1–6 in **C** to the answers. Listen to check.
☐ Yes, my sister lives there.
☐ Miguel Hernández.
☐ No, I don't. I live with my girlfriend, Monica.
☐ In Madrid. I work there. It's an amazing city!
☐ Yes, I am. I'm from Valencia.
☐ Alaska.

Common mistakes

does
Where /your mother lives?

do
Do you like soccer? Yes, I ~~like~~.

3 Pronunciation: Question intonation and silent *e*

A ▶ 2.9 Look at AS 2.9 on p. 161. Then listen again and notice how the intonation in each question goes up (↗) or down (↘) at the end. Complete the rules.
1 If it is a *Yes / No* question, the intonation usually goes _____.
2 If it is an information question, the intonation usually goes _____.

B Complete 1–5. Take turns asking and answering the questions. Use the correct intonation.
1 _____ you have a brother?
2 _____ many cousins do you have?
3 _____ 's your mother's name?
4 _____ 's your father's name?
5 _____ they live near you?

C 🗣 **Make it personal** Write two more *Yes / No* questions and two more information questions. In pairs, take turns asking and answering them. Use the verbs to help you.

| have | go | like | live | play (sport) | study | travel | visit |

Do you live in an apartment? *Yes, I do.* *Where exactly do you live?*

2.4 When do you check your phone?

1 Listening

A ▶ 2.10 Listen to Miguel talking to a friend about these three photos on his phone. How many questions do you hear? Who are the people?

B 👤 **Make it personal** In pairs, show photos of your family and say who they are. Ask two questions about your partner's photos.

This is my brother, Carlos.   *Where does he live?*   *He lives in Canada.*

And who's this woman?   *This is Susan, my brother's wife.*

2 Reading

A ▶ 2.11 Read the webposts about cell phone habits and match 1–7 with the correct name. Listen to check.

☐ Ruben   1 checks her phone at breakfast.
☐ Jan   2 doesn't check his phone at dinner.
☐ María's boyfriend   3 doesn't check her phone.
☐ Lucía's friends   4 send messages all day.
☐ Gerry   5 checks his phone at dinner.
☐ Milton's son   6 checks his phone when they go out.
☐ Greg's mom   7 doesn't look at his phone when he eats.

Cell phone habits

I never look at my phone when I eat. It's a really bad habit. Oh, except when I have lunch alone!

Ruben, New York

I sometimes check my phone at breakfast. My dad gets really mad!

Jan, Los Angeles

My boyfriend occasionally checks his phone when we go out together. I think that's OK.

María, Mexico City

My mom never checks her phone, so I have to call her!

Greg, London

My friends send me WhatsApp messages all day, so I always check my phone every five minutes – when I'm not busy.

Lucía, La Paz

My boss always sends me messages late at night, so I often need to check my phone at dinner.

Gerry, Boston

My son plays games and uses apps on his phone all the time, so he's always on it. I insist he stops at dinner!

Milton, Rio de Janeiro

B 👤 **Make it personal** In groups, talk about when you and your family / friends check your / their phones. Who checks it when they eat and why? Who has the best reason?

I check my phone at breakfast because my boss gets up at 5:00 a.m.

My brother checks his phone every two minutes - I think he's addicted to it!

🎵 *I will never say never! (I will fight)*
I will fight till forever! (make it right) **2.4**

③ Grammar Frequency adverbs

A Complete the grammar box.

> **1** Put the frequency adverbs in the correct place in the chart.
>
> always   never   occasionally   often   sometimes   usually
>
> ___ ___ ___ ___ ___ ___
>
> **2** Number these statements 1-4 from least to most frequent.
> a My sister sometimes goes to the theater. ☐
> b I never go to the gym. ☐
> c My parents always go to work. ☐
> d My friends often go to parties. ☐
>
> **3** Does the frequency adverb go before or after the verb?
>
> → **Grammar 2C** p. 140

⚠️ **Common mistakes**

I always
~~Always I~~ go to the movies on the weekend.

B 🗣 **Make it personal** Do a class survey.
1 Read the questions and put a ✓ in column 1 for you.
2 In pairs, ask and answer. Put your partner's answers in column 2.
3 Report your answers to the class. Which are good / bad habits? Who has the best habits?

Do you ...	never		occasionally		sometimes		often		usually		always	
	1	2	1	2	1	2	1	2	1	2	1	2
take selfies every day?												
check your phone every five minutes?												
text during a conversation?												
make voice calls?												
leave voicemail?												
use earphones (to listen to music)?												
use your phone in the bathroom?												
turn off your phone at night?												

💬 *Carla always texts during a conversation — even with her teacher!*

💬 Eduardo never uses earphones to listen to music. He listens on the bus. That's a bad habit!

25

2.5 How old are you?

ID Skills Reading Asking for personal information

A Read the interview with Ginny Lomond and complete questions 1–9 with the correct verb.

freshfaces.com

Pop singer Ginny Lomond answers your questions about her life.

1. What _____ your full name?
2. Interesting! And how old _____ you?
3. Don't worry! Do you _____ a pet?
4. Where _____ you live?
5. And where _____ your family live?
6. Great! Do you _____ any brothers or sisters?
7. I see. And what _____ you do on the weekend?
8. OK, and what time do you _____ to bed on weekdays?
9. And our final question! _____ you exercise regularly?

☐ No, I don't exercise. Well, only occasionally (when I walk Boston). I'm a little lazy!
☐ Well, my mom lives in Paris, and my dad lives in L.A.
☐ I sleep a lot and occasionally go for a walk. And I never work on Mondays, so I often go to bed late on Sundays.
☐ I usually go to bed at 11 p.m. from Monday to Thursday, but I sometimes go to parties!
☐ Yes, I do. I have a dog called Boston. I love him!
☐ I live in Paris.
☐ Virginia Marie Lomond.
☐ No. I'm an only child.
☐ Umm … OK, I'm 23.

B ▶ 2.12 Match the questions to the answers in the interview. Listen to check.

C Find and underline five examples of frequency adverbs in the interview.

D In pairs, ask and answer *How often …?* questions with the *go* activities in **1A** on p. 18.

How often do you go to the gym?   I never go to the gym!

E 🗣 **Make it personal** In pairs, role-play the interview.
A: Ask the nine questions.
B: Give your own true answers.
Then change roles.

⚠ **Common mistakes**

How often
~~With what frequency~~ do you …?

2.5 How do you celebrate your birthday?

♪ *Music's got me feeling so free, We're gonna celebrate.*

ID in Action Celebrating

A Match the phrases with photos 1–6.
- ☐ Congratulations!
- ☐ Enjoy your meal!
- ☐ Happy birthday!
- ☐ Happy New Year!
- ☐ Have a good trip!
- ☐ Merry Christmas!

B ▶ 2.13 Listen to check. Try to remember the answers.

C What do you say on occasions 1–6? Practice saying the phrases with a partner.
1. before dinner
2. at a wedding
3. on your mom's birthday
4. before a friend goes on vacation
5. on December 25th
6. on January 1st

D 🔴 **Make it personal** Write how often you / other people do the activities in the chart on each special occasion.

always   never   occasionally   often   sometimes   usually

	On your birthday	At Christmas	On New Year's Eve	On the Day of the Dead	At Carnival	Another celebration?
have a special meal at home						
go to a restaurant						
drink and eat special food						
have a party						
give and receive gifts						
wear special clothes						
go to bed late						
spend a lot of money						
dance and sing						
go to the cemetery						

E In small groups, compare answers. Find one thing you do differently.

I always have a special meal at home on my birthday.

I never eat at home on my birthday. We usually go to a restaurant.

⚠ Common mistakes

~~On~~
At Christmas Day = a specific day or date.

~~At / For~~
~~On~~ Christmas = a festive period.

Writing 2 A personal email

🎵 *You are not alone, I am here with you, Though we're far apart, You're always in my heart.*

A Read the email and number the things that Matt does in order.
- ☐ have breakfast
- ☐ do homework
- ☐ take a shower
- ☐ have dinner
- ☐ go to a café
- ☐ leave home
- ☐ go for a run
- ☐ wake up
- ☐ get up
- ☐ get dressed

B Imagine you are Matt. Answer the questions.
1. What's your full name?
2. Where does your family live?
3. Do you have any brothers or sisters?
4. When do you get up?
5. Do you exercise regularly?
6. What do you do after school?
7. When do you do your homework?
8. What do you usually do on the weekend?

✓ Write it right!

In positive sentences and most questions, put the frequency adverb before the verb. In negatives, put *always*, *usually*, or *often* after the auxiliary (*don't* or *doesn't*).

C Read **Write it right!** Decide where you would put the adverb in the following sentences and questions.
1. Jack goes to the gym on the weekend. (**often**)
2. My brother doesn't remember my birthday. (**always**)
3. Serena checks her phone in class. (**never**)
4. Where do you spend your summer vacation? (**sometimes**)
5. Veronica's friends don't go out on weekday evenings. (**usually**)
6. Do you play games when you should be studying? (**occasionally**)

D Note your own answers to the questions in **B**.

E 👤 **Make it personal** Write a similar email about your typical week (about 150–180 words).

Before	Use your notes in **D**. Think of some extra information, too.
While	Use frequency adverbs in the correct position.
After	Exchange emails with a partner and give feedback.

To: **James**
Subject: My typical week
Today at 13:23
All Mail

Hi there,

I live in Hamilton, New Zealand, with my parents and sister. A typical weekday for me starts early. I get up at 6:00 a.m., but I **usually** wake up before that. I **often** go for a run first thing. After my run, I **always** take a shower and have breakfast, then I get dressed and get ready for school. I leave home at 8:00 a.m.

After school, I don't **usually** go straight home. I **sometimes** go to a café to meet my friends, to the park to play football, or I **occasionally** go to the gym. We have dinner at 6:00 p.m., but my dad **doesn't always** get home in time to eat with us. I **usually** do my homework after dinner, between 6:30 p.m. and 8:30 p.m. Then I watch TV, play video games, or message my friends. I **never** go to bed before 10:00 p.m.

On the weekend, I get up late and then go out with my friends. We **usually** go to the beach, or to a party. And we **sometimes** visit my cousins in Auckland. Sunday evenings are normally very quiet.

That's a typical week for me. What about you?

Matthew James McCarthy (Matt)

2 The critic

1 Before watching

A Complete 1–6 with a word from the box.

critic   guitar   show
record   reviews   voice

1 Genevieve plays the _____ and writes songs.
2 The _____ listens to music and writes about it.
3 The _____ are great.
4 She's a good singer and has a very beautiful _____.
5 Rory has a video camera to _____ the show.
6 Andrea and August are at the café to watch Genevieve's _____.

B Guess and circle the correct answer. Compare in pairs, then watch to check.

1 **Rory uses / The critic uses / Both of them use** a video camera.
2 **Rory wears / The critic wears / Both of them wear** glasses.
3 **Rory listens / The critic listens / Both of them listen** to the music.
4 **Rory sits / The critic sits / Both of them sit** at a table in the café every day.
5 **Rory drinks / The critic drinks / Both of them drink** a cup of coffee.
6 **Rory writes / The critic writes / Both of them write** at a table.

Who do you think uses a camera?

I guess they both use a camera. Do you agree?

2 While watching

A Watch again. Order the sentences 1–10 as you hear them, then complete them. Who says each one?

☐ She plays Monday and Saturday _____ 8 and 9:30.
☐ Excuse me. Do you _____?
☐ Except he needs _____ give me a good review.
☐ Rory _____ you're a great singer anyway.
☐ She's not the _____ one that thinks so.
☐ She's the _____ there is, for sure.
☐ That was _____, cuz. Good job!
☐ This is _____ life!
☐ You are crazy. He _____ do that.
☐ You have _____ amazing voice.

B Order Rory's routine 1–5.

☐ He sits down.
☐ Rory comes to the café.
☐ He orders coffee.
☐ He waits for Genevieve to take his order.
☐ He drinks his coffee and dreams.

C What's Genevieve's schedule? Check (✓) (M) in the morning, (A) in the afternoon, or (N) at night.

Genevieve ...	M	A	N
practices the guitar for two hours.			
takes a class.			
goes to work.			
gets up.			
writes a song.			
sings at the café.			

3 After watching

A How do they feel? Complete 1–4 with the adjectives.

annoyed   excited   nervous   upset

1 Genevieve feels _____ about the show.
2 The critic's very _____ at Rory.
3 Andrea's _____ to hear Genevieve's music.
4 Rory's _____ and leaves the café.

B How many hits does Genevieve's video get online?
☐ 9   ☐ 19   ☐ 95   ☐ 99

C 🔘 **Make it personal** Check (✓) the kinds of reviews and reports you read. In pairs, ask and answer about them.

☐ books / art / museums   ☐ news / weather
☐ movies / TV shows / theater   ☐ sports / local events
☐ products / online services   ☐ hotels / vacations
☐ fashion / music / dance

Do you ever read book reviews?

Sometimes, but only online. Never in newspapers.

29

R1 Grammar and vocabulary

A **Picture dictionary.** Cover the words on these pages and use the pictures to remember:

page	
6	8 countries and nationalities
11	11 personal objects
13	10 colors
15	5 short dialogues for photos 1–5
18	8 *go* activities
20	10 morning routine verbs
22	25 family members
27	6 phrases for special occasions
158	16 picture words for vowels

B **Make it personal** In pairs. A: Spell sentences 1–3. B: Write the sentences. Change roles for 4–6. Are the sentences true for you?

1 MY CITY IS INTERESTING.
2 I REALLY LIKE JAZZ.
3 I AM FROM NEW YORK CITY.
4 MY FAVORITE COLOR IS GREEN.
5 MY FAMILY IS LARGE.
6 I OFTEN READ NEWSPAPERS.

C ▶R1.1 Complete with verb *be*. Use contractions where possible. Listen to check. Then role-play in pairs.

Receptionist: What _____ your name?
Sandy: Sandy Clark.
Receptionist: _____ you American?
Sandy: No, I _____ Canadian.
Receptionist: Where in Canada _____ you from?
Sandy: Vancouver.
Receptionist: That _____ a nice place. What _____ your address?
Sandy: 76, Burton Road.
Receptionist: And what _____ your email address?
Sandy: saclark@hotmail.com
Receptionist: Thank you. Here _____ your key. Room 89.

Good afternoon. Can I help you?

Hi! Yes, please. I have a reservation.

D Play *Draw it, name it!* A: Go to p. 8 Exercise D and draw six objects for B to name. Change roles. B: Go to p. 11 Exercise A and draw six objects for A to name.

How do you say this in English?
Sorry, I don't remember.
It starts with "u".

E **Make it personal** Complete the questions with *do* or *does*. In pairs, ask and answer.

1 What _____ you do on your birthday?
2 _____ you give gifts to your family at Christmas?
3 _____ you eat a special meal on Christmas Eve?
4 _____ your mother usually have a party on her birthday?
5 What _____ you do at weddings in your culture?
6 What _____ your brother (or sister) do on New Year's Eve?

F Match responses a–h to phrases 1–8. Then practice in pairs. Say a phrase for your partner to respond.

1 Thank you.   a Good, thanks.
2 Who's this?   b Not much.
3 What's new?   c It's Jackie.
4 Congratulations!   d Thanks!
5 How're you?   e You're welcome.
6 See you later.   f Purple and white.
7 How old are you?   g Bye for now.
8 What color is your house? h 17.

G Correct the mistakes. Check your answers in units 1 and 2.

1 Are you colombian? Yes, I'm. (2 mistakes)
2 That is a umbrella ridiculous. (1 mistake)
3 David loves her girlfriend. (1 mistake)
4 John go to home after school. (2 mistakes)
5 My girlfriend has 20 close parents. (1 mistake)
6 At what time you go to school? (2 mistakes)
7 My father work in the city. (1 mistake)
8 At Saturday, my mom don't study usually. (3 mistakes)
9 My brother has 25. (1 mistake)
10 When he works? (2 mistakes)

30

Skills practice

🎵 *But just because it burns, doesn't mean you're gonna die, You gotta get up and try.*

R1

A Match the phone phrases. Read the text to check.
1 send — online
2 make — a meeting
3 take — the dictionary
4 go — a (text) message
5 use — a photo
6 organize — a call

> Everyone has a phone, but people have different attitudes to their phones. Let's take a look at when people check their phones.
>
> 1 "I check it all day all the time. I _____ send messages and post things when I'm at school."
>
> 2 "I don't have a cell phone. I think they ruin conversation! I _____ use my friend's phone to make calls."
>
> 3 "I _____ check my phone for news updates. I _____ read on my phone when I have free time. My parents _____ get annoyed when I look at my phone or go online during meals."
>
> 4 "I _____ check my phone for work. I _____ make calls from the car to talk with clients or organize meetings for the day."
>
> 5 "I _____ use my phone to take photos and to post them on social media all day long! All my friends do the same. I don't want to be different."

B 👤 Make it personal | Complete the sentences with the best frequency adverb: *always, usually, often, sometimes, occasionally,* or *never*. Are you similar to any of the people in **A**?

> I'm similar to 5. I don't want to be different from my friends.

C ▶ R1.2 Listen to a student. Circle the correct number.
1 She's **17 / 70** years old.
2 Her town is **13 / 30** km from Barcelona.
3 She has **6 / 9** brothers and sisters.
4 She gets up at **6 / 8** a.m.
5 It takes **15 / 50** minutes to get to school.

D ▶ R1.2 Listen again and answer 1–5.
1 What's her name?
2 Where does she live?
3 Where does she study?
4 When does she go to the movies?
5 Who are her favorite actors?

E In pairs. **A:** Describe family 1. **B:** Describe family 2.

F 👤 Make it personal | Complete the chart by checking (✓) the activities you do. Compare with a partner. Any big differences?

How do you spend your weekends?	Friday	Saturday	Sunday
get up early			
go shopping			
go to bed late			
meet friends			
play sports			
watch TV			

G 👤 Make it personal | Complete 1–6 and compare your answers in pairs. Any unusual choices?
1 _____ is a rich young person.
2 _____ is a great American actor.
3 _____ is an excellent song.
4 _____ is an interesting new movie.
5 _____ is a cool small piece of technology.
6 _____ is a fantastic big city.

H In pairs, role-play this situation.
A: You're a guest at a hotel. You want to leave your bag in their security box. Pay by credit card.
B: You're the receptionist. Ask A for this information: name; ID card number; room number; description of bag; contents of bag; credit card number.

I 👤 Make it personal | Question time.
In pairs, practice asking and answering the 12 lesson titles in units 1 and 2. Use the book map on p. 2–3. Where possible, ask follow-up questions, too. Can you comfortably ask and answer all the questions?

> Are you Canadian?   No, I'm Peruvian.
>
> Ah, I see. Are you from Lima?

3.1 What's the weather like?

1 Vocabulary Weather

A ▶3.1 Listen to a meteorologist and complete the weather chart.

	the sun	a cloud	wind	fog	rain	snow
noun	☀	☁	〰	≡	💧	❄
adjective	sunny					
verb					to rain	to snow

Common mistakes

raining
It's ~~rain~~ in this photo.
It's usually rainy /
It usually rains
It's ~~usually rain~~ in January.

B Study the chart and complete the rules.
1 To form adjectives from weather nouns, add _____.
2 For consonant-vowel-consonant words, double the final _____ and add _____.

C Match the temperature words to the correct thermometer position, a–d.
☐ cold ☐ cool ☐ hot [c] warm

D In pairs, use the photos and thermometer to remember the 10 adjectives.

E ▶3.2 Listen and identify the two photos the students are talking about.

F 🔴 Make it personal In pairs, do the same. Take turns describing the photos and guessing the place. Use *it's* + adjective.

In photo 7, it's really snowy. I think it's somewhere in the mountains in the U.S.

I disagree. The houses aren't American. Maybe it's Europe.

32

I want to know, Have you ever seen the rain, Comin' down on a sunny day? **3.1**

2 Listening

A ▶3.3 Listen to the TV show and number the places in the order you hear them, 1–5. Why do they say the weather is unusual?

	Usually	Now
☐ the Alps		
☐ the Amazon rainforest		
☐ the Atacama Desert		
☐ Cancún		
☐ Chicago		

> **Common mistakes**
> How's the weather ~~like~~?
> It's
> ~~Is~~ really hot.
> windy
> It's ~~winding~~.

B ▶3.3 Listen again and complete the chart in **A** with adjectives / words for each place.

C Complete the three questions from the show.
1 And _____'s the weather in Chicago?
2 _____'s the weather usually like there?
3 What's it _____ this year?

D 🔴 **Make it personal** In pairs, ask and answer about the weather in the photos, and in your city / country. Use the model and point to the photos as you ask.

> What's the weather usually like in the Amazon rainforest?   It's rainy.

> And how is it now?   It's very dry.

33

3.2 Are you busy at the moment?

1 Vocabulary Everyday actions

A ▶3.4 Match photos 1–6 to the actions. Then listen to Maddie make five phone calls. Which action don't you hear?

- [ ] buying groceries
- [ ] doing homework
- [ ] running in the park
- [ ] cooking dinner
- [ ] riding a bike
- [ ] talking on a landline

B ▶3.4 Listen again and match the person to the activity that they are doing.

Maddie _____   Susan _____   Rita _____
Eli _____   Michael _____

C 🔴 Make it personal In pairs, say which of the activities you do and which you don't do. When do you do them? Can you name other activities that you do?

> *Riding a bike?*   *Yes, I do this on Saturdays when it's warm and when it's not raining.*

2 Grammar Present continuous (1)

A ▶3.5 Listen to Maddie's last phone call. Answer the questions.
1 Why is she looking for company?
   - [ ] To have dinner.
   - [ ] To go to a sports event.
   - [ ] She's feeling lonely.
2 How does the story end?
   - [ ] She gets depressed and cries.
   - [ ] She finally finds a friend who is free.
   - [ ] She does her homework.

> ⏱ **Common mistakes**
> *are doing*
> What ~~you do~~ now?
> *Are you*
> ~~You are~~ studying English?
> Yes, I ~~do~~.
> *am*

B Complete the grammar box.

> 1 Complete the examples with the verb *be*.
>   ⊕ She _____ talking on the phone. → Subject + *be* + verb *-ing*
>   ⊖ I _____ _____ running. → Subject + *be* + not + verb *-ing*
>   ? What _____ they doing? → Question word + *be* + subject + verb *-ing*
>
> 2 Delete the incorrect options.
>   Use the present continuous for actions that happen **every day / at the moment / sometimes**.
>
>   Don't pronounce the /g/ in the *-ing* ending. It's /ɪn/ or /ɪŋ/ (like *king* and *ring*).

→ **Grammar 3A** p. 142

C ▶3.6 In pairs, listen to the sound effects. What are the people doing?
1 They're cooking.   3 _____   5 _____
2 She _____   4 _____   6 _____

D Look back at p. 20. Take turns testing a partner about Jake's morning routine.
> *What's Jake doing in "e"?*   *He's taking a shower.*

E 🟢 Make it personal Role-play a conversation like Maddie's. **A:** You're calling five friends to do something. **B:** You're A's friends. Make different excuses. Change roles.
> *Hi, this is Marcia. Are you busy?*   *Yes, I'm cooking dinner!*   *OK, call you later!*   *Bye!*

⏱ **Common mistakes**
I'm
~~I~~ working on a new project.

🎵 *Winter, spring, summer or fall, All you've got to do is call and I'll be there, yeah, yeah, yeah, You've got a friend.*

3.2

③ Reading

A ▶3.7 Study the months. Is the stressed syllable the same (S) or different (D) in your language? Listen to check. Then say your birthday month.

January ☐   February ☐   March ☐   April ☐   May ☐   June ☐   July ☐
August ☐   September ☐   October ☐   November ☐   December ☐

> **Common mistakes**
> *in March*
> My birthday's ~~on march~~.

B Read the extract from an encyclopedia and:
1 write the seven missing months.
2 circle the names of three more seasons in paragraph 1.
3 find two more seasons in paragraph 2.
4 find the names of one continent and two countries.
5 find the words to complete the compass.

Four seasons or two?

Countries with a temperate climate, like the ones in Europe and North America, have four defined seasons: hot (summers) in June, _____, and August; cold winters in December, January, and _____, with heavy snow in some countries; cool, windy falls in September, _____, and November, and warm springs in _____, April, and _____.

In contrast, tropical regions, especially around the equator, have only two seasons: the dry season and the rainy season. So, in places like India, West Africa, Central America, the north of South America, and the north coast of Australia, the rainy season is in their winter (_____, July, and _____), and it's accompanied by very high temperatures.

C ▶3.8 Listen to and read the encyclopedia extract. Any pronunciation surprises?

D In pairs, answer the questions.
1 Which months correspond to which seasons in your country?
2 What's your favorite season? What's the weather like in your favorite season?
3 Say three things you usually do in your favorite season, and three you don't.

> *I don't usually go out a lot in the rainy season. I watch a lot of TV!*

E 🗣 **Make it personal** In groups. Think of a month and season. Mime an activity that you usually do in that season. Your group guesses what you are doing, the month, and the season.

> *Are you swimming?*   *Yes, I am.*   *Is it summer?*   *Yes.*
>
> *Is it December?*   *Yes, it is.*

35

3.3 What are you doing these days?

1 Listening

A ▶3.9 Listen and identify the people in the pictures.
1 Marisa 2 Jennifer 3 Kevin 4 Steve

B ▶3.9 Listen again. True (T) or False (F)? Correct the false statements.
1 Marisa is working at the moment. _____
2 She's studying art. _____
3 She's living with her parents. _____
4 She's dating Kevin. _____

2 Grammar Present continuous (2)

A Complete the grammar box.

> 1 Put the questions in the correct column.
> *What are you doing these days?   Are you studying art?*
> *Are you dating Kevin?   Where are you living?*
>
> | Wh-? | Yes / No? |
> |---|---|
> | | |
> | | |
>
> 2 Which question type (*Wh-* or *Yes / No*) uses which structure?
>   a verb *be* + subject + verb *-ing* _____
>   b question word + verb *be* + subject + verb *-ing* _____
>
> 3 Delete the incorrect option.
> We use the present continuous to talk about things happening:
>   a right now.   b in the past.   c around now.

➔ Grammar 3B p.142

B Put the words in order to make questions. Ask and answer with a partner. Talk about other people, too.
1 you / are / doing / what / ?
2 working / where / you / are / ?
3 are / what / studying / you / ?
4 at home / living / you / are / ?
5 dating / are / you / ?

> What are you doing at the moment?   Nothing special. I'm working a lot during the week.
>
> Oh, really! Where are you working?   I have a new job now! At the aquarium. I feed the fish!

Common mistakes
Are you coming
Do you come for coffee?
are you going
Hi! Where do you go?
I go home.
'm going

C 🔴 Make it personal Invent a new personality! Ask and answer questions. Use the ideas below. Who has the most interesting life?

do a lot of exercise   go out a lot   listen to music   read   sleep well
speak more English   spend a lot of money   watch (a show on) TV

♪ Don't stop me now, I'm having such a good time, I'm having a ball.

3.3

③ Reading

A Match the technology problems 1–5 to photos a–e.
1. identity theft
2. addiction
3. consumerism
4. isolation
5. violence

B Read the online debate and match the person to the problem in **A** they write about.

 Sammy
What do you think of technology?

 Marsha
It's dangerous. Social media companies are changing the way we see privacy. Everyone is getting access to our personal information.

 Lucinda
I don't like a lot of the new video games. They're getting more violent and it makes people act more violently.

 KoolKat
People are going out less and spending more time alone with technology. We don't know our neighbors.

 Dadofthree
People today are becoming obsessed with things! They want new clothes, new cars, new electronic devices, and they can buy it all online.

 BBaxter
My kids are spending more and more time on their devices and online, especially on social media. I don't know what to do. They panic when they don't have their phone with them. They just want to look at their phones.

C ▶3.10 Now listen and check your answers. Who do you most agree with? Practice saying what they say.

D 🗣 **Make it personal** What do you think the problems with technology are? List the problems in **A** in order of importance. Say why. Who agrees with you?

What's your most important problem?

Isolation. People are spending too much time on their phones.

I agree. Communities are changing. I don't know my neighbors.

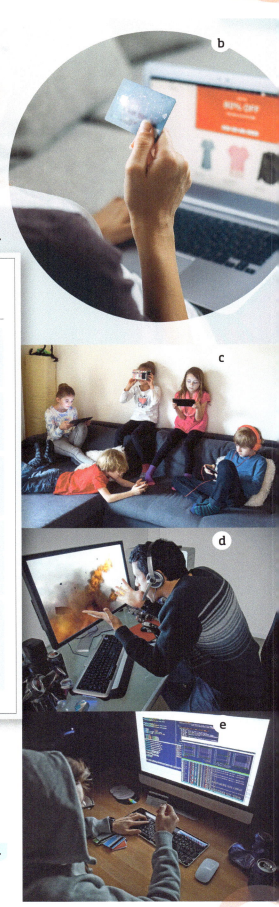

37

3.4 What do you do after school / work?

1 Grammar Simple present vs. present continuous

A In pairs, can you recognize the celebrities in the photos? What do they do?

Who's this?   *I think this is Naomi Watts.*   *What does she do?*   *I think she's a movie star.*

B Match photos 1–6 to these actions. What are the people doing? In pairs, take turns asking and answering.

- ☐ walk the dog
- ☐ listen to music
- ☐ watch a game
- ☐ watch a show
- ☐ shop
- ☐ drive a car

What's Steph Curry doing?   *He's listening to music.*

C Complete the grammar box.

1 Read the paragraph and for sentences a–d write SP (simple present) or PC (present continuous).

Jack Morley is a celebrity journalist. ᵃ He usually works from 8 a.m. to 5 p.m. in his office ☐, and ᵇ he talks to his editor every morning ☐. ᶜ This week, Jack's doing a lot of different things ☐. ᵈ Right now he's interviewing a famous actor ☐.

2 Match the rules.

a Use the present continuous to
b Use the simple present to

1 talk about routines.
2 talk about something happening around now.
3 describe actions in progress now.
4 describe habits.

→ **Grammar 3C** p. 142

Common mistakes

I'm living
I'm live at home at the moment.
I like
I'm liking this movie.

♪ I'm giving it my all, but I'm not the girl you're taking home, oh, I keep dancing on my own.

3.4

D For each of the people in A, imagine what they usually do at these times and what they are probably doing right now or, more generally, around now.

	1	2	3	4	5	6
8:00 a.m.						
12:30 p.m.						
7:30 p.m.						

> I think Steph Curry usually gets up before 8:00 a.m. Right now, I guess he's training. More generally, he's probably working on a new charity project.

E 🎧 **Make it personal** Make a timeline of what you usually do during a regular day. Are there any things that you are doing around now that you don't usually do?

> I go to college on weekdays. But, I'm training for a marathon, so now I'm running every morning.

> At the moment, I'm taking an English class at a language school.

⚠️ **Common mistakes**
every morning
I'm running ~~all the mornings~~ at the moment.

② Listening

A In pairs, share what you know about these celebrities.

> That's George Clooney. He's married to a Lebanese-British lawyer.

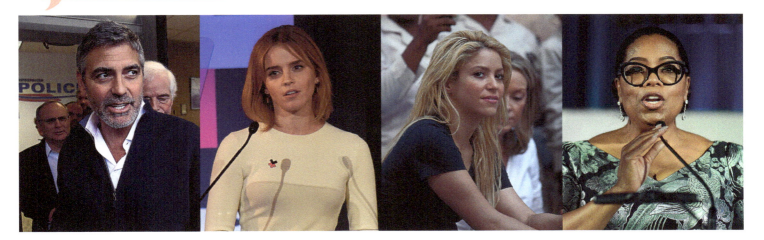

B ▶ 3.11 Listen to Jack Morley talk about celebrities. Does he think celebrity activists are a good thing or a bad thing?

C ▶ 3.11 Listen again and check (✓) which causes are mentioned.
- ☐ cyberbullying
- ☐ clean water
- ☐ corruption
- ☐ peace
- ☐ climate change
- ☐ animal rights
- ☐ education for girls
- ☐ women's rights
- ☐ racism

D ▶ 3.11 In pairs, complete these sentences. Then listen to check.
Celebrities _____ _____ a lot of publicity to these causes and people _____ _____ more money on the causes. But what do celebrities know about these _____ ?

E 🎧 **Make it personal** What do you think of celebrity activists? Give a reason.

> I think Emma Watson is a good person and she helps people.

> Yes, but she is an actor, not a politician.

> But she's smart!

3.5 Why are you learning English?

ID Skills   Analyzing your English

A Read the introduction to the questionnaire. Are questions 1–2 True (T) or False (F)?
1 We know exactly how many people speak English in the world.
2 The questionnaire is for the authors of this book.

> Approximately 25% of the world speaks or is now learning to speak English, and this number is rapidly increasing. Please help the ID team to learn more about our users' motivation and experiences. Complete our questionnaire, checking (✓) all relevant answers, and let us know.

1 Why are you learning English?
a ○ for my current or future job ○ for school ○ for college
b ○ for pleasure ○ I love learning languages
c to communicate: ○ online ○ in writing ○ speaking
d ○ to communicate with other people face-to-face
e ○ to pass an exam
f ○ to travel
g ○ to emigrate
h other (what?) _____

2 Which are the three most important for you? Number them 1 to 3.
a ○ grammar   d ○ listening   g ○ writing
b ○ vocabulary   e ○ speaking   h ○ all equally
c ○ pronunciation f ○ reading   important

3 Which items in **2** do you find the most difficult?
_____

4 How often do you do these things in English outside class? Mark them:
E=Every day   V=Very often   S=Sometimes   O=Occasionally   N=Never
a ○ read   e ○ watch TV / movies
b ○ study   f ○ speak to people face-to-face
c ○ write / send messages   g ○ communicate online
d ○ listen to music / the radio h ○ other (what?) _____

5 What do you like about your ID classes?
a ○ the coursebook
b ○ the workbook
c ○ the ID student's learning platform
d ○ my classmates
e ○ other? _____

Common mistakes

I need ~~learn~~ English ~~for~~ pass my course.
    to   *to*

I have ~~learn~~ English ~~to~~ my job.
    to   *for*

I'm needing to get a new ~~work~~.
                      job

B Answer the questionnaire. In pairs, compare your answers.

C **Make it personal** In groups, explain your answers to the questionnaire.

> I'm learning English for many reasons. I need it in school. I'm taking some exams in English.

> I'm working at an international company at the moment. I need to talk to people from many different countries in English.

3.5 Are you thirsty?

🎵 *So one last time, I need to be the one who takes you home.*
One more time, I promise after that, I'll let you go.

ID in Action   Making offers

A ▶ 3.12 **Listen to two friends and answer 1–5.**
1. What time is it?
2. What's Linda working on?
3. When does she have to finish it?
4. How many more pages does she have to write?
5. Is she tired?

B ▶ 3.12 **Listen again and write Mark's three questions. Guess what happens next.**

> Maybe Linda decides to go home.   Yeah. Perhaps. Or maybe she doesn't …

C ▶ 3.13 **Listen to the next part of the conversation to check. What does Linda want?**

D ▶ 3.12 and 3.13 **Listen again and match the formal and informal expressions.**

Grammatical English		Informal English
1 Are you tired?	a	Yep. / Yeah.
2 Do you want to go home?	b	Cookie?
3 Yes.	c	You tired?
4 Would you like a cookie?	d	Wanna go home?

E ▶ 3.12 and 3.13 **Listen again. In pairs, role-play the dialogue using the picture clues.**

Mark		Linda
☕	→	U/1?
✅	→	✅ ⚫ no 🥄
🍔 too?	→	❌
🍪 ?	→	❌
☕⬆	→	U R GREAT !

⚠️ **Common mistakes**

'm not
I ~~don't have~~ hungry, but I'm
~~with thirst.~~
    Would
~~Do~~ you like a drink?

F ▶ 3.14 **Match the questions and offers. Listen, check, and practice the different responses.**

Questions	Offers	Responses
Are you bored?	Do you want a sweater / to use my jacket?	Yes, please. Great!
Are you cold?	Do you want a sandwich? / Wanna cookie?	Sure. Why not?
Are you hot?	Would you like a coffee / to go home?	Yep / Yeah!
Are you hungry?	Would you like a drink?	Uh-huh, just …
Are you thirsty?	Do you want a cold drink / some ice cream?	No, thanks.
Are you tired?	Maybe you need a vacation / a new job?	No, really, I'm fine.
Are you stressed?	Wanna go out for a coffee / a walk?	That sounds great!

G 👥 **Make it personal**   In pairs. **A:** Mime an adjective from the chart in **F**. **B:** Ask a question and make an offer from the chart or one of your own. **A:** Respond.

> Are you bored? Wanna read my newspaper?

Writing 3 A language profile

🎵 *Louder, louder, And we'll run for our lives, I can hardly speak I understand.*

A Read two student profiles and label the diagrams.

Personal details

My name's Marta and I'm 20.

Why are you learning English?
I often travel _____ other countries, so English is very important. I want _____ go _____ Los Angeles and India.

Which aspect of language is the most important for you?
_____ me, the most important thing is speaking. I need _____ communicate _____ people when I go on vacation.

What aspects of language are you good / bad at?
I'm not good _____ writing. I know how to say English words, but they are difficult _____ spell! I enjoy speaking _____ people and exchanging opinions. I'm good _____ talking – in fact, I never stop!

How do you practice English outside your classroom?
I use the Internet all the time, so I read the news _____ English and talk _____ my cousins in Canada online.

Personal details

My name's Mateo and I'm 24 years old.

Why are you learning English?
English is important <u>for my career</u>. (I often have to read) documents <u>in English</u> and I hope to get a promotion soon. Also, I'm going <u>to New York</u> next month!

Which aspect of language is the most important for you?
<u>For me</u>, the most important thing is pronunciation. It's often difficult to <u>communicate with</u> people because they don't understand me – and I don't understand them. It's very frustrating!

What aspects of language are you good / bad at?
I'm <u>terrible at</u> speaking! I want to <u>speak to</u> other people, but it isn't easy. When I'm reading, I go slowly and use a dictionary. I think I'm <u>good at</u> vocabulary, especially because many English words are <u>similar to</u> Italian words!

How do you practice English outside your classroom?
I don't have much time to practice <u>at home</u> because I work a lot. I occasionally watch American movies and read the subtitles. I need to practice more!

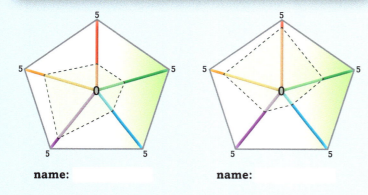

name: _____   name: _____

B Read **Write it right!** In Mateo's profile, circle five more words / phrases followed by *to* + infinitive.

> ✓ **Write it right!**
>
> *To* + infinitive and prepositions are often difficult to remember. When you read, try to notice phrases, and then use them when you write and speak.

C Notice the <u>underlined</u> preposition phrases in Mateo's profile. Complete Marta's profile with *to, for, with, at,* and *in.*

D Complete the diagram in **A** for you. Rate each aspect of language 0–5.

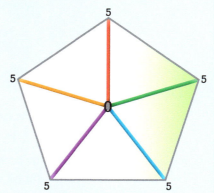

E 🔵 **Make it personal** Write your language profile in 80–120 words.

Before	Use the diagram in **D** and the questionnaire on p. 40.
While	Use prepositions carefully.
After	Read a partner's profile and draw their diagram.

3 Storm tracker

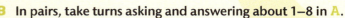
ID Café

1 Before watching

A What are they doing? Look at the photo and check (✓).

August	Daniel	
		is looking in a bag.
		is sitting on a sofa.
		is standing behind the sofa.
		is using a computer.
		is checking a list.
		is holding a smartphone.

B Cover the chart. In pairs, take turns describing the scene.

The two guys are at home. August is …

C Put the words in the correct column. Watch and number them 1–10 in the order you hear them.

| clouds | fast | heavy | lightning | storm |
| steady | filmmaker | video disc | shaky |
| zoom lens |

Weather	Equipment	Adjectives	Job

2 While watching

A What's Daniel doing? Write Yes (Y) or No (N).

Daniel's …
1 carrying the equipment.
2 reading the list.
3 carrying the keys.
4 driving the car.
5 keeping the camera steady.
6 applying for an internship.
7 filming the storm.
8 introducing his storm tracker.

B In pairs, take turns asking and answering about 1–8 in **A**.

Is Daniel filming the storm?

No, he's not. August is filming the storm.

3 After watching

A Write True (T) or False (F). Correct what's false.
1 August uses the tripod.
2 Daniel's talking slowly into the microphone.
3 The storm's coming at 3:33.
4 The clouds behind Daniel aren't moving fast.
5 There's no lightning in the sky.
6 It's raining while August is filming.
7 They're making the video before the rain comes.
8 Daniel drops the microphone.
9 August keeps the camera steady.
10 Daniel is disappointed with the video footage.

B Order the story 1–9. In pairs, take turns saying a line of the story at a time.

☐ Daniel and August get wet and go home.
☐ Daniel and August are checking their list and Daniel asks about the tripod.
☐ Daniel invents a storm tracker app.
☐ Daniel checks if August can hear him.
☐ August doesn't bring the tripod.
☐ Daniel gets annoyed with August about the video footage quality.
☐ August and Daniel drive to the field.
☐ August films Daniel while the storm's passing over them.
☐ There's lightning just before they make the video.

C ⬤ **Make it personal** In groups, talk about photography. Who uses their camera the most?
1 In an average week, how many photos and videos do you take?
2 What do you usually take photos and videos of?
3 Do you ever use a tripod or selfie stick?
4 What's your best recent photo or video?
5 How often do you share or upload photos?

It depends. I like to take photos of nature.

I don't normally take videos, except when I'm out with friends.

♪ No time for losers, 'cause we are the champions of the world.

4.1

1 Vocabulary Sports

A ▶4.1 **Match the sports with photos 1–7. Try to pronounce them. Then listen to part of a sports show to check. Find two reasons why they are in two groups.**

- [1] basketball ✓
- [ ] volleyball
- [ ] tennis
- [ ] soccer
- [ ] cycling (bike riding)
- [ ] swimming
- [ ] running

Maybe it's because the first four we play …

B **Listen to and repeat what your teacher says only if it's true for you. In groups, do the same.**

Teacher: I like tennis.   *Some students: I like tennis.*

C ▶4.2 **Listen to more of the sports show and check (✓) in A the five sports Mac mentions. Can you remember the six countries, too?**

D ▶4.2 **Listen again and match the times to the places.**

1 9:00   [ ] the Igloo
2 9:30   [ ] North Park
3 10:00   [ ] the Olympic Arena
4 10:30   [ ] the Olympic Stadium
5 11:00   [ ] the Central Courts

✓ Common mistakes

I love the games.
I don't like the fruit.
I hate the soccer.
Don't use *the* with plural nouns or uncountable nouns or to talk about things in general.

E ▶4.2 **Say the places in D. What's the difference in the pronunciation of *the*? Complete the rules with *th*/ə/ ("the") or *th*/iː/ ("thee"). Listen to check.**
1 Before a vowel sound, pronounce *the* _____.
2 Before a consonant sound, pronounce *the* _____.

F ▶4.3 **Listen and repeat the noun with *th*/ə/ or *th*/iː/ before you hear the beep.**
Airport: *The airport.*

G ▶4.4 **Listen to four interviews and order the sports you hear, 1–6. Which sports don't you hear?**

- [ ] baseball
- [ ] football
- [ ] golf
- [ ] hockey
- [ ] rugby
- [ ] skateboarding
- [ ] skiing
- [ ] soccer
- [ ] surfing
- [ ] table tennis

H 👤 **Make it personal** **Answer in pairs. Which sports in this lesson …**
1 need a ball?
2 need a net?
3 can you practice in the ocean?
4 are your favorite to watch / practice?
5 are your country usually good at in the Olympics?
6 are the most and the least dangerous?

Our country is usually good at …   *For me, the most dangerous is …*

In my opinion, the least dangerous sport is …

45

4.2 Can you drive a tractor?

1 Grammar Can: Yes / No

A ▶ 4.5 It's Mark's first day at the gym. Listen and complete the form.

B ▶ 4.5 Listen again and complete the grammar box. Notice the weak pronunciation of *can* in the questions.

> **Common mistakes**
> Can you play soccer well?
> ~~You can play well the soccer?~~

	Yes / No? with can	Short answers
1	_____ you run two ki**lo**meters?	No, I _____.
2	_____ you swim?	Yes, I _____.

→ **Grammar 4B** p. 144

C Ask two friends the same questions and complete this form with ✗ or ✓. Now ask about four other sports. How many *Yes* answers can you get?

D 🔴 **Make it personal** Match the verbs to the noun groups. Ask your classmates about these abilities using *Can …?* Find someone who can do each one well.

play   drive   sing
speak   cook

Can you cook Chinese food? *No, I can't. Not at all! Can you?*
Yes, I think so. But not very well.

the pi**a**no	English	in **har**mony	a **trac**tor	Chinese food
the gui**tar**	French	karaoke well	a truck	Mexican food
the **sax**ophone	Chinese	a song in a		French food
the drums	**Ger**man	third language		Japanese food
the vio**lin**				

46

② **Listening**

🎵 *Heal the world, Make it a better place, For you and for me, And the entire human race.*

4.2

A What do you know about Malala Yousafzai? In pairs, say what you know about her, or make guesses. Read the article to check.

Malala Yousafzai

is probably the world's most famous Pakistani. Her 2009 blog about life under the Taliban for the BBC, and her activism made her many enemies. She was shot in the head when she was only 15 years old. But she survived, and in 2012 won the Nobel Peace Prize. She lives in the UK now and campaigns for education for girls across the world.

B ▶ ◉4.6 Watch / Listen and order the words as you hear them, 1–8. Which items are in the photos?

- [ ] book
- [ ] child
- [ ] education
- [ ] pen
- [ ] powerful
- [ ] solution
- [ ] teacher
- [ ] weapons

C ▶ ◉4.6 Watch / Listen again and write Malala's speech. In pairs, compare. Check your answer in AS 4.6 on p. 162.

D ◉4.7 58% of English comes from Latin, so you can guess many English words, like words with the suffixes -tion and -sion. Do you recognize the words below? Read the pronunciation rule. Then try to pronounce the words correctly. Listen to check.

With suffixes -tion and -sion, always stress the syllable before the suffix.

action	corruption	motivation
combination	expression	opinion
conversation	information	organization
cooperation	isolation	question

E 👤 **Make it personal** Which of the items in the photos in **B** can best change the world? In pairs, order them 1 to 4 from the most to the least powerful. Then compare with another pair. Do you agree?

> *Number 1?*   We think it's a teacher.

> *We believe a book can be more powerful.*   For us, that's number 2.

47

4.3 What languages can you speak?

1 Grammar Can: ⊕ ⊖ and Wh- ❓

A ▶4.8 Listen to the interviews. Complete sentences 1–6 with *can* or *can't*. Listen again to check.

1 I _____ dance very well, but my wife _____. She's a very good dancer.
2 My father _____ cook really well. His food is delicious.
3 My best friend _____ play baseball or volleyball. He doesn't like team sports.
4 I _____ skate, but I _____ ski at all. Skiing is too difficult!
5 My friends _____ play soccer very well. They play every weekend.
6 _____ you do any martial arts? Yes, I _____. What _____ you do? Tae Kwondo.

B Complete the grammar box.

> 1 We use *can* to talk about ability. Study the examples in **A** and circle the correct option.
>   a *Can* goes **before** / **after** the main verb in a sentence.
>   b *Can* **changes** / **doesn't change** form in the 3rd person.
> 2 Complete rules c and d with the words.
>
>   can   Wh- question word   person   verb
>
>   c To form a *Yes* / *No* question with *can* use: _____ + _____ + _____.
>   d To form a *Wh-* question with *can* use: _____ + _____ + _____ + _____.
>
>   ➡ **Grammar 4B** p. 144

C ▶4.8 Listen again and notice the pronunciation of *can* and *can't*. In pairs, practice pronouncing the sentences in **A** correctly.

D 🟢 **Make it personal** Write three true and three false sentences about you and people you know and their abilities. In pairs, decide which are true and which are false.

Anna can play the guitar well.   *I think that's false. Anna can't play the guitar at all!*

E 🟢 **Make it personal** *Can* is also used for requests. Read and choose the three most useful phrases for 1) everyday life and 2) English classes. Compare with a partner. Any similarities?

Can you help me?   Can I say it in (my language)?
Can you translate this?   Can I open the window?
Can you speak louder?   Can I park here?
Can you spell it, please?   Can I have a little more (coffee)?
Can you close the door?   Can I go home now?
Can I go to the bathroom?

② Reading

🎵 *Filled with all the strength I found, There's nothing I can't do! I need to know now, Can you love me again?*

4.3

A ▶ 4.9 Listen, read, and match photos a–f to six of the abilities.

Ten Keys to 21st Century Success

To fly high in the modern world, certain abilities are essential. Here are our top 10 in no particular order:

1. to Google efficiently
2. to understand directions quickly
3. to cook the basics
4. to remember names
5. to use simple tools
6. to speak two common languages
7. to dress appropriately
8. to bargain well
9. to make friends easily
10. to make a good first impression

B Many adverbs are formed adjective + -ly, e.g., *probably, finally, especially, certainly, exactly*. Underline four examples in **A**. Can you find an irregular one, too?

C Use these symbols to mark the list in **A** according to your ability. Then interview a partner about their abilities. What can they do well?

✗✗ = I can't at all.　✗ = I can't very well.　✓ = I can.　✓✓ = I can very well.

Can you use simple tools?　*No, I can't! I always ask my mom to help me.*

⚠️ **Common mistakes**

I can type ~~quick~~ *quickly*.
I can't cook ~~good~~ *well*.

D 👤 **Make it personal** Choose the five most important abilities for you.

I'm at school and I don't have a job, so my most important are …

③ Listening

A ▶ 4.10 Listen to a job interview. Circle the job that Maddie wants.
   a babysitter　a journalist　a secretary　a teacher

B ▶ 4.10 Listen again and complete with *can* or *can't*.
1. Maddie _____ speak Spanish very well.
2. She _____ play volleyball and tennis but not very well.
3. She _____ text fast.

C 👤 **Make it personal** In pairs, think of a job. Write a list of questions to ask about abilities for that job. You can use AS 4.10 on p. 163 to help you. Now interview another pair. Do you give them the job?

Can you speak Portuguese fluently?　*No, I can't.*　*Sorry. We're looking for a Portuguese teacher!*

4.4 Are you an organized person?

1 Vocabulary Clothes

A ▶ 4.11 Listen to the fashion show. Who's JKK? Do you like the designs?

Today's designs for tomorrow's world.

B ▶ 4.11 Match 1–16 to the clothes items.

- ☐ a silver belt
- ☐ a brown blouse
- ☐ blue boots
- ☐ a gold jacket
- ☐ a yellow dress
- ☐ black sandals
- ☐ a purple shirt
- ☐ orange shorts
- ☐ a pink skirt
- ☐ beige socks
- ☐ a blue suit jacket
- ☐ blue shoes
- ☐ a green T-shirt
- ☐ a white tie
- ☐ gray sneakers
- ☐ blue suit pants

C Cover the words in **B**. In pairs, describe the four models.

D 🅜 **Make it personal** Look at what your classmates are wearing for a minute. In pairs, take turns describing without looking and guessing. Now do the same with photos of people on your phone.

> She's wearing a red sweater.   Is it Carmen?

⚠ Common mistakes

She always wears a green shirt and ~~a~~ gray pants to school.
He's ~~using~~ *wearing* a suit.
She has two ~~jeans~~ *pairs of jeans*.

> I have about twenty pairs of jeans.

> Twenty? I only have three pairs.

2 Reading

A Do you have a lot of clothes? Describe your closet to your partner.

B Answer the title question from the forum. Then read the three posts and match them to pictures 1–3.

Victoria: _____   Kyle: _____   Tanya: _____

Can organized and messy people live together?

It's not impossible, but it's difficult. At home, it's only me and my husband. My clothes and shoes are always organized, but his are not! Sometimes I get angry because he is messy and I'm neat, but usually it's OK. **Posted by Victoria**

I confess: I don't like to share — it's too difficult! So my wife and I have separate closets. I have more things than she does, so my closet is enormous and hers is not. We are both clean and organized, but the problem is our kids! We clean our room, but we never look in theirs! Their rooms are messy and full of dirty sports equipment — balls, rackets, skis, etc. Horrible! It's hard for people who are very different to live together, but if you're family you can do it! **Posted by Kyle**

In my house, we don't say "mine" or "yours". Everything is ours. Our house is small, and a little disorganized, but we like it like that. We share space and clothes. We occasionally have a conversation like this: "Whose sweater is this?" "It's yours!" "No, it's yours!" That's a big advantage of living with your twin sister! We are very similar. I can't live with people who are different from me. **Posted by Tanya**

♪ Oh, oh, oh, Sweet child o'mine,
Sweet love o'mine.

4.4

C Complete the sentences with the names from the forum and *her* or *his*.
1 ____ lives with ____ sister.
2 ____ lives with ____ husband.
3 ____ lives with ____ wife and children.
4 ____ is different from ____ children.
5 ____ can share easily.
6 ____ can't share at all.

D ▶4.12 Match the four underlined words in **B** with their opposites below. In pairs, try to pronounce all the words in **B** with pink syllables. Listen to check. Any surprises?

calm   clean   disad**van**tage   **sep**arately

E 🟢 **Make it personal** Who are you more similar to: Victoria, Kyle, or Tanya? Find one person in the class who is like you and one person who is different.

I share a room with my sister, but I'm organized and she isn't. I think I'm similar to Victoria.

3 Grammar   Possessive pronouns

A ▶4.13 Look at the highlighted phrases in **2B**. Complete the grammar chart. Listen to check. Then answer questions 1–3.

	Possessive adjectives	Possessive pronouns
This is	my closet	mine
	your closet	
	her	
	his	
	our	
	their	

1 How many possessive pronouns end in *s*?
2 Is the final *s* pronounced /s/ or /z/?
3 Read the rules and complete the dialogue with *hers*, *mine*, or *whose*.
   Use *Whose?* to ask about possession.
   Use a possessive pronoun to replace a possessive adjective + noun.
   A: _____ phone is that?
   B: I think it's _____. (not "her phone")
   C: No, it isn't. It's _____. (not "my phone")
4 Rewrite the dialogue above using *phones* instead of *phone*.

➜ **Grammar 4C** p. 144

⏰ **Common mistakes**
These glasses are ~~the~~ mines.
Whose pen is this?
~~Of who~~ is this pen?
                      's
It's ~~of~~ Maria.

B In groups, take turns describing one item of clothing in the classroom to the rest of the group. Then point and say whose it is.

It's a green and white T-shirt. Whose is it?   *It's hers!*   *No!*   *It's his!*   *Yes.*

C 🟢 **Make it personal** Write your own post for the forum. Use the prompts to help you. Compare in pairs. How are you similar and how are you different?
I live with …
My room is …
I (don't) share my room …
I am (an organized / a messy …) person.
I (can / can't share) things (easily).
I think people who are different (can / can't) live together.

I share a room with my brother. We have a lot of things, and our room is very messy!

51

4.5 Do you like spas?

Skills — Reading for details

A Quickly look at the text and answer the questions.
1 Where do you think it's from? ☐ the Internet ☐ a book ☐ a magazine
2 What is it? ☐ a poster ☐ an ad ☐ a blog

{ALL YOURS}

Do you like healthy food and healthy living?

All Yours is the perfect place for you. There, in the same ultra-modern center, you can find:

† **Super Salon** with unisex hair stylists, manicurists, and pedicurists available from 8 a.m. to 10 p.m., seven days a week.

† **Natural Foods** restaurant that serves high-quality, healthy foods, specially prepared by our expert chefs and nutritionists. Open from 7 a.m. to midnight daily.

† **World Boutique** with unique fashion designs from around the world for everybody, young or old.

† **Marvelous Me** massage suite. Our fantastic therapists can eliminate all your stress.

† **Giant Gym.** A great place to stay in shape and keep your heart and muscles healthy.

B Read the text. True (T) or False (F)?
1 All Yours is a shopping mall.
2 The hair stylists work on Sundays.
3 It's possible to eat, buy clothes, de-stress, and exercise there.
4 It's for women and men.
5 Five different professions are mentioned.

C Find the words in the text that mean:
1 the opposite of different =
2 in good health =
3 take away =
4 continue to be =

Yes, the suffix -ist isn't stressed in English.

D ▶ 4.14 In pairs, pronounce the words with pink syllables. Listen to check. Any surprises?

E 🔴 **Make it personal** In pairs, plan the perfect day at All Yours. Tell another pair about your day. Who has the best day?

We arrive at 7 a.m. and go for breakfast at Natural Foods.   *We go to the gym first at 7 a.m.*

4.5 What shoe size are you?

♪ *You can't always get what you want. But if you try sometimes, yeah, you might find you get what you need.*

in Action   Shopping for clothes

A ▶ 4.15 Listen to the dialogue and complete 1–4. Predict how it ends.
1 The man's at a …
2 He wants …
3 The color he wants is …
4 The size he wants is …

B ▶ 4.16 Listen to part two of the dialogue and answer the questions.
1 Who's the sweater for?
2 Why does he want it in blue?
3 Do you think the salesclerk is good at his job?

C Listen to ▶ 4.15 and ▶ 4.16 again and find:
1 the preposition we use before colors.
2 the verb that means "to test clothes on your body".
3 the name of the room where we go to do this.

Common mistakes

these pants / them
Do you like ~~this pants~~?
                    do / like them
                          Yes, I ~~like~~.

D ▶ 4.17 Listen to and complete a short version of the dialogue. What three changes do you need to make if he asks for jeans?

Salesclerk: Can I _____ you?
Jason: Yes, please. Can I _____ the _____ in the window?
Salesclerk: Sure! What _____? We have it in _____, blue or _____.
Jason: _____, please.
Salesclerk: All right. What _____?
Jason: Extra _____.
Salesclerk: _____ small in blue? OK, just a _____, please. Here you _____.
Jason: Thanks. Can I _____ it on?
Salesclerk: Sure. The fitting _____ are over _____.

E In pairs, practice the dialogue in **D**. Use other clothes items from this unit. Be careful with singular and plural forms.

F ▶ 4.18 Punctuate the rest of the dialogue. Listen to check. Then cover and practice from the photos.

Jason: nothanksjustthesweaterhowmuchisit
Salesclerk: fortynineninetynine
Jason: greatheresmycreditcard
Salesclerk: thankyoupleaseenteryourpinnumber
Jason: hereyougo
Salesclerk: heresyourreceipthaveanicedaybyejackson

G **Make it personal**   Go shopping!
1 In groups, discuss the questions.
   What do you wear …   a to school / work?   c on the weekend?
                         b to go to a party?   d to a job interview?
2 In pairs, go shopping for clothes for one of the situations in 1.
   A: You're the customer. **B**: You're the salesclerk.

Hi! I like these black shorts. How much are they?

53

Writing 4 A job application

Sweet home Alabama,
Where the skies are so blue
Sweet home Alabama,
Lord, I'm coming home to you.

A Read the job ad and find the names of
1 the company advertising the job.
2 the job the ad is for.
3 the person you have to write to.

Make this your best ever summer – at 50 States Summer Camp!

Would you like to: ✪ have the chance to visit the U.S.? ✪ spend the summer working with young people? ✪ teach a sport or a skill that you are passionate about? ✪ make amazing new friends and have a fantastic time?

If so, send an email to: rebecca@50states.com. Tell us about you, your skills, your likes and dislikes, and why you want to be a counselor at 50 States Summer Camp. Include any questions you'd like us to answer. One of our team will contact you for a phone interview.

To: **Rebecca**   Today at 16:03
Subject: **50 States Summer Camp Counselor**   All Mail

Dear Rebecca,

I am an 18-year-old high school graduate from Granada in the south of Spain. Right now, I'm working in a local restaurant. I really enjoy it, but I'm planning to go to college in the fall to study sports science.

I can play most sports. I play soccer very well, and I'm a good swimmer, so I'm sure I can teach those. I'm teaching my younger brother to play guitar at the moment – I play the guitar quite well, but I can't sing at all, unfortunately. I'm good at languages – in addition to Spanish, I speak English and French.

As a person, I'm quite organized and tidy, and I'm not good at living with other people if they are messy. I like music and reading, but I really love being outside and spending time with my friends. I also love food. I can cook, but not very well. I hate shopping.

This summer, I want to do something that is connected to my future studies and also uses my skills. I like helping other people, and I love to see them enjoying the same things I do. And, of course, I'd love to visit the U.S.!

I look forward to hearing from you.

Sincerely,
Ana Sofía Reynoso

B Read Ana's email and underline.
1 her job and current plans.
2 five things she's good at and one she's not.
3 the languages she speaks.
4 two positive adjectives to describe her.
5 five things she does well and one she doesn't.
6 five reasons she wants the job.

⊘ Write it right!

Use a variety of intensifying adverbs with adjectives, adverbs, or verbs – *not ... at all, not very, quite, really, very.*

C Imagine you want to apply for the job in **A**. Note your answers to 1–6 in **B**.

D 🔵 **Make it personal** Write a similar email applying to 50 States Summer Camp (about 180–200 words).

Before	Use your notes in **C**. Add any information you think is important.
While	Use intensifying adverbs to describe your skills and likes.
After	Exchange emails with a partner. Decide who is the best candidate.

4 Whose action hero?

 Café

1 Before watching

A Look at the photo. Where are Andrea and Lucy?
☐ at a tennis court   ☐ at a gym   ☐ at a stadium

B 👤 **Make it personal** Check (✓) which are true for you and correct the others.
1. I can sing.
2. I can do acrobatics.
3. I can do martial arts.
4. I can box, but I can't do kickboxing.
5. I can dance, but I can't sing.

C 👤 **Make it personal** In pairs, take turns asking and answering *can / can't* questions about the activities in B.

> Can you sing?   No, I can't. What about you?

2 While watching

A Check (✓) the correct columns according to what Lucy, Andrea, and Paolo say.

	Andrea		Lucy		Paolo	
	can	can't	can	can't	can	can't
talk to Paolo						
still join the class						
dance						
do gymnastics						
be in Lucy's film						
text their number						
help someone catch up						

B Write True (T) or False (F). Correct the false sentences.
1. Lucy and Andrea can't take Paolo's kickboxing class.
2. Andrea's film project is due next week.
3. Andrea can't do gymnastics.
4. Martial arts is Andrea's taste.
5. Andrea is flexible but not so strong.
6. Lucy says that Andrea can't be in her film.
7. Paolo offers to help Lucy catch up before the class starts.

3 After watching

A Complete this extract.

Lucy: Hey, what's up?
Andrea: I want to take an exercise class. Summer _____ coming.
Lucy: Summer? I _____ only think about _____ action film. It's due next week.
Andrea: _____ class should I take? Jim _____? Marie _____? Whose class _____ best?
Lucy: You see that guy over there? Whatever _____ taking.
Andrea: Martial arts? That's _____ taste, not mine.
Lucy: I think I just found _____ new action hero. Let's go.

B Complete with *his / her / their* or noun + possessive *'s*.
1. Lucy's going home to work on _____ script.
2. Paolo's taking Andrea to _____ class.
3. Lucy can text Paolo _____ number.
4. Andrea can also be in _____ film.
5. Lucy and Paolo are sharing _____ cell phone numbers.

C 👤 **Make it personal** In groups of three, design your ideal superhero. What can she / he do? Present her / him to the class.

> This is our superbot, Queen Fantastic! She can do many things …

55

R2 Grammar and vocabulary

A **Picture dictionary.** Cover the words on these pages and use the pictures to remember:

page	
32–33	10 weather adjectives
34	6 everyday actions
35	4 seasons
37	5 technology problems
38	6 activities
45	7 sports
46	5 abilities
48	6 talents
50	16 clothes items
53	the clothes store dialogue
158	10 picture words for diphthongs

B Complete with weather adjectives and the month (January = 1, December = 12).
1 In <u>December</u> (12), New York is usually very c <u>o l d</u>.
2 Lima is a very c _ _ _ _y city in _____ (7).
3 London is a r _ _ _y place in _____ (10).
4 The coast of Canada is very f _ _ _y, especially in _____ (1).
5 It is s _ _ _y in Bariloche. Winter there starts in _____ (5).
6 Sydney's very s _ _ _y, especially in _____ (2).
7 La Mancha's very w _ _ _y in _____ (8).

C **Make it personal** Match questions 1–3 to answers a–c. Complete a–c so they're true for you.
1 What's the weather usually like in your city in July?
2 Is it raining at the moment?
3 Does it usually rain a lot in your city?
  a _____, _____ does / doesn't.
  b It _____ and _____.
  c _____, _____ is / isn't.

D **R2.1** Circle the correct alternatives. Listen to check. In pairs, role-play the dialogue.
Tyler: Hello?
Shannon: Hi, Tyler. This is Shannon. What **are you doing / do you do**?
Tyler: Oh, hi, Shannon. I **'m watching / watch** the football game.
Shannon: Oh? Who **'s playing / plays**?
Tyler: You **'re kidding / kid**, right?
Shannon: Tyler, you **'re knowing / know** that I **'m not liking / don't like** sports.
Tyler: OK, OK ... the Cowboys and the Giants **'re playing / play** right now.
Shannon: And who **'s winning / wins**?
Tyler: The Giants, 31–14. They **'re always winning / always win**.
Shannon: Sorry to hear that! Um ... **do you want / are you wanting** to go out later?

E Cross out the incorrect response.
1 When are you leaving?
  a Every day at 6:30 a.m.
  b Tomorrow morning.
  c In two weeks.
2 Can I see the sweater in the window?
  a Sure. What size are you?
  b Sure. How much is it?
  c Sure. What color do you prefer?
3 Here are the boots.
  a I like them very much.
  b How much are they?
  c Can I try it on?
4 Are you busy on the weekend?
  a No problem.
  b Yes, I'm working both days.
  c Not really. What are you doing?
5 Can you sing?
  a I can, but not very well.
  b Not at all.
  c Yes, I am.
6 What sports can you play?
  a No, I can't.
  b I can play volleyball and tennis.
  c I can't play any sports.

F **Make it personal** In pairs, ask and answer 4–6 in **E**. Make more questions by changing the verbs.

G **Make it personal** Play *Last-to-first Race!* In pairs, take turns saying these in reverse order.
1 The months: December, ...
2 The days of the week: Sunday, ...
3 Numbers 1 to 20: Twenty, ...
4 Your daily routine: I go to bed, ...
5 Your phone number: ...

H Correct the mistakes. Check your answers in units 3 and 4.
1 How's the weather like in June? (1 mistake)
2 Is raining in Patagonia at the moment. (1 mistake)
3 Do you hungry? You would like a sandwich? (2 mistakes)
4 Is usually cold in december in Canada. (2 mistakes)
5 My daughter studying at the moment. (1 mistake)
6 What your best friend is doing now? (2 mistakes)
7 He go to Europe the next month. (2 mistakes)
8 Patty can to play very well the tennis. (3 mistakes)
9 Gloria is using a blue jeans. (2 mistakes)
10 Of who are these shoes? They're of Jane. (3 mistakes)

Skills practice

🎵 *California girls, we're undeniable, Fine, fresh, fierce, we got it on lock, West Coast represent, now put your hands up.*

R2

A ▶R2.2 Listen to an interview with Paralympic swimmer Ricky Pietersen and number the questions in the order you hear them, 1–4.
- [ ] What else do you like doing when you're not swimming or watching your team?
- [ ] Do you like soccer?
- [ ] What is your next big challenge?
- [ ] So, Ricky, what's your favorite sport?

B ▶R2.2 Listen again and correct 1–5.
1. Well, I love singing, of course.
2. Yes, I love to watch my team win.
3. I like to read to young kids with disabilities.
4. I'm working hard to prepare for the next Panamerican Games.
5. I have to beat my own result.

C Match words 1–3 from the interview to their meanings a–c.
1. Paralympics
2. disability
3. beat the record

a. a physical or mental condition that limits a person's activities
b. to do better than the last person to hold the record
c. the Olympic Games for athletes with disabilities

D In pairs, use the information in **A** and **B** to role-play the interview. Then change roles.

So, here I am with today's guest, Paralympic swimmer, Ricky Pietersen. Hi, Ricky!

E ▶R2.3 Read the blog page. Can you guess the missing words? Listen to check your answers.

My name is Cristina Valenzuela and I ¹_____ twenty-three years ²_____. I live in Santa Monica, California. My parents are originally ³_____ Chile, so I ⁴_____ speak Spanish very well. I love sports. I go to the beach every day, and I surf and swim when the ⁵_____ is good. It's usually very ⁶_____ and sunny here! I love it!

I'm ⁷_____ very casual person. I usually ⁸_____ shorts and a T-shirt during the day and jeans at night. When it's cold, I sometimes wear ⁹_____ sweater, but I don't like it very ¹⁰_____. I prefer to wear summer ¹¹_____. Write me an email! Maybe we ¹²_____ go to the beach together next summer.

F Answer questions 1–4 about her blog page.
1. Why can Cristina speak Spanish well?
2. What sports does Cristina usually practice?
3. What's the weather usually like in Santa Monica?
4. What does she like to wear?

G 🔴 **Make it personal** Question time.
In pairs, practice asking and answering the 12 lesson titles in units 3 and 4. Use the book map on p. 2–3. Where possible, ask follow-up questions, too. Can you comfortably ask and answer all the questions?

What's the weather like? *It's very hot again!*

Is it windy, too? *No, it's not. No wind, no rain, only sun!*

5.1 Is there a mall in your area?

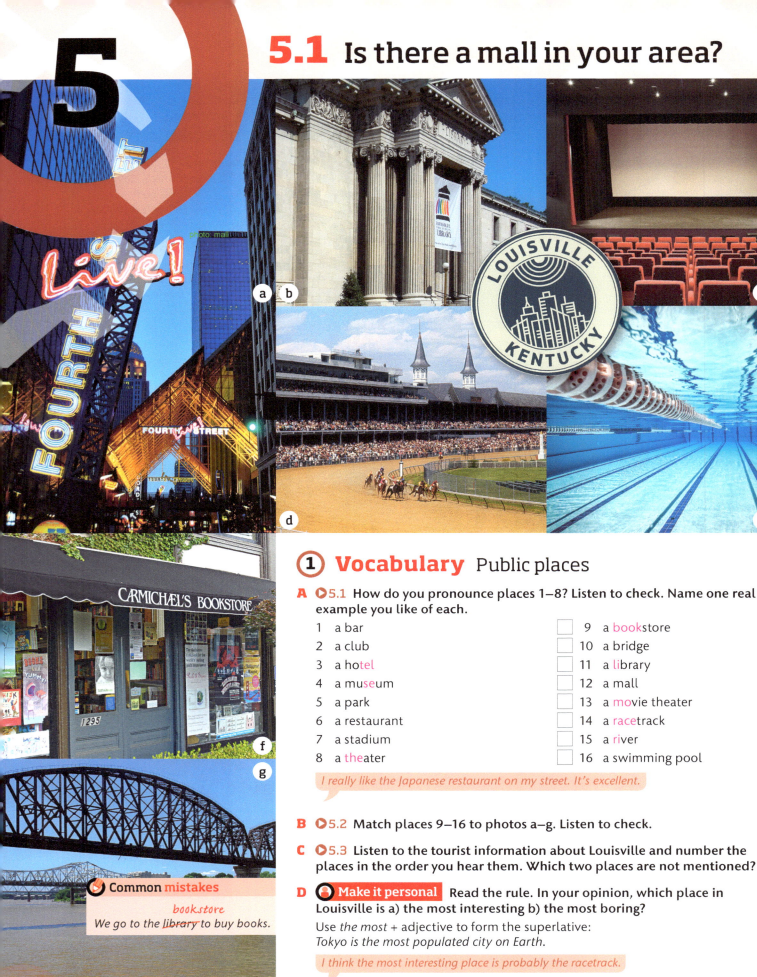

1 Vocabulary Public places

A ▶5.1 How do you pronounce places 1–8? Listen to check. Name one real example you like of each.

1. a bar
2. a club
3. a hotel
4. a museum
5. a park
6. a restaurant
7. a stadium
8. a theater

☐ 9. a bookstore
☐ 10. a bridge
☐ 11. a library
☐ 12. a mall
☐ 13. a movie theater
☐ 14. a racetrack
☐ 15. a river
☐ 16. a swimming pool

I really like the Japanese restaurant on my street. It's excellent.

B ▶5.2 Match places 9–16 to photos a–g. Listen to check.

C ▶5.3 Listen to the tourist information about Louisville and number the places in the order you hear them. Which two places are not mentioned?

D 🔴 **Make it personal** Read the rule. In your opinion, which place in Louisville is a) the most interesting b) the most boring?

Use *the most* + adjective to form the superlative:
Tokyo is the most populated city on Earth.

I think the most interesting place is probably the racetrack.

⚠️ **Common mistakes**
~~bookstore~~
We go to the ~~library~~ to buy books.

58

🎵 There's nothing you can't do,
Now you're in New York.
These streets will make you feel brand new
Big lights will inspire you.

5.1

2 Grammar *There is / are* ➕➖❓

A ▶5.4 Complete 1–4 in the grammar box with *a, any, are,* or *no*. Listen to check.

	➕	➖	❓
Singular	There is a ...	There is no ...	Is there a ...?
Plural	There are ...	There are no ... There aren't any ...	Are there any ...?

1 There _____ seven museums downtown.
2 There's _____ famous racetrack at Churchill Downs.
3 There aren't _____ swimming pools in downtown Louisville.
4 There are _____ unfriendly people.

➡ Grammar 5A p. 146

⚠ **Common mistakes**

There's a
~~Have one~~ famous baseball stadium in Louisville.

There are no
~~No have~~ swimming pools in downtown Louisville.

B In pairs, each ask four *Can you ...?* questions about Louisville using these verb phrases.

eat out   go to the beach / the movies / the theater
go shopping / skiing / swimming   stay in a nice hotel   watch horse racing

Can you go skiing?

No, you can't. There aren't any mountains.

C 👤 **Make it personal** Compare your hometown to Louisville. Find at least five differences.

In Louisville there's a baseball stadium, but there's no baseball stadium in my hometown.

3 Reading

A ▶5.5 Read and complete the brochure with *a, an, is, are,* or *no*. Listen to check.

Come to **Markville!**

It's _a_ great place to live. There _____ two museums and _____ great public library. There _____ also a movie theater, so you can see _____ movie if you want. There's _____ mall, but there _____ lots of cool shops and _____ historical bank. Markville has two hotels: there's _____ old traditional hotel and there _____ a new modern one, so you can choose where you stay. There are _____ clubs, but there _____ a bar inside one of the hotels. For food lovers, there _____ two delicious restaurants, one French, the other Mexican, and _____ interesting café, too. Downtown is for pedestrians, so there are _____ cars to ruin the peace. People are warm, the weather is, too. The food is great, so see you soon!

B Which picture is Markville, 1 or 2? Explain.

C Work in pairs. **A**: Look at the pictures and answer.
B: Don't look! Ask **A** questions to find four differences between the two pictures.

Is there a ...?   *Are there any ...?*

D 👤 **Make it personal** In groups, describe a town or neighborhood you know. Is it a great place to live?

_____ is a nice place to live. There is a big mall downtown and so many things to do.

5.2 What are your likes and dislikes?

1 Vocabulary Free-time activities

A ▶5.6 Listen to Sandy and complete her blog post with the words.

cleaning   cooking   eating   going   playing   shopping   watching

Home | **About me** | **Archive** | **Contact me**

Sandy's blog

Here are the 10 things I do most every week in order of how much I like them. ☺

1. _____ video games ☐
2. going out with friends ☐
3. _____ ☐
4. _____ out ☐
5. blogging ☐
6. _____ to work ☐
7. _____ with a friend ☐
8. working out / exercising ☐
9. _____ TV ☐
10. _____ the house ☐

What about you? Are you like me? ☺

B ▶5.7 Match her blog activities to photos a–j. Listen and write the number of the activity in the chart.

😍 love	😃 like	😐 don't mind	😟 don't like	🤢 hate
1				

C 🔴 **Make it personal** Make a chart like the one in B and write 10 activities. Compare in pairs. Find two things you have in common.

I hate going to the dentist, and I don't like exercising.   *We both love dancing salsa.*

2 Grammar like / love / hate / not mind + verb -ing

A Match the statements that have similar meanings.

1. I like to clean the house.
2. She hates swimming.
3. He doesn't like to clean the house.
4. I don't mind swimming.

a. Swimming is OK with me.
b. He hates cleaning the house.
c. She doesn't like swimming.
d. I like cleaning the house.

60

🎵 *I don't mind spending every day,*
Out on your corner in the pouring rain,
Look for the girl with the broken smile.

5.2

B Use the statements in **A** to help you complete the grammar box.

> Choose the correct answer.
> a With *love, like, hate,* use:
>   1 *to* + verb   2 verb *-ing*   3 both are possible
> b With *not mind,* use:
>   1 *to* + verb   2 verb *-ing*   3 both are possible
>
> ➡ **Grammar 5B** p. 146

Common mistakes
               driving
I hate ~~drive~~ in traffic.
                    driving
I don't mind ~~to drive~~ at night.

C Order the words to make sentences.
1 like / soccer / on / don't / I / watching / games / TV / .
2 friend / loves / go / to / movies / my / best / the / to / .
3 mind / in / don't / shopping / I / malls / .
4 my / hate / out / work / sisters / to / .

D 👤 **Make it personal** Change the sentences in **C** so they are true for you. Find someone who has the same sentences as you.

> *I don't mind watching soccer on TV.*   *I don't mind either!*

③ Pronunciation

A ▶5.8 Listen to the people talking about household chores. Match sentences 1–4 to photos a–d.
1 I don't <u>mind</u> cleaning the <u>bathroom</u>.
2 I love <u>ti</u>dying my room.
3 I hate doing the <u>laun</u>dry.
4 I like <u>wash</u>ing the dishes.

B ▶5.8 Listen again. <u>Underline</u> the stressed words in sentences 2–4. Are pronouns, articles, and possessive adjectives normally stressed or unstressed?

> *I don't mind washing the dishes, but I hate doing the laundry.*

C 👤 **Make it personal** Change the sentences in **A**, 1–4, so they are true for you. Compare with a partner. Do you agree?

④ Listening

A Read the ad for the show. Guess the answers to questions 1–3.
1 How old is she?
2 What does she love to do?
3 Who does she want to be like?

B ▶5.9 ▶ Watch the video and check your guesses. Do you think she has talent?

C 👤 **Make it personal** Imagine you're on a talent show. Introduce yourself and say what you love doing and who you want to be like.

> *Good evening, everybody, I'm Sam, and I love to rap. I want to be like Jay-Z.*

The *Got Talent* franchise is a very popular TV talent show. There are versions of this show in more than 50 countries. Before the contestant shows his or her talent, there is an introduction to the person.

61

5.3 What do you like doing on vacation?

1 Vocabulary Vacation

A ▶ 5.10 Listen to and repeat 1–7, but say *I like* or *I don't like* before the activities.

Subject		Emily	Josh	You
1	camping			
2	cooking			
3	dancing			
4	hiking			
5	eating out			
6	buying souvenirs			
7	swimming			
8	visiting museums			
9	kayaking			
10	reading novels			
11	sightseeing			
12	snorkeling			
13	sunbathing			
14	taking a class			

B ▶ 5.11 Match activities 8–14 to the photos. Listen to check.

C ▶ 5.12 In pairs. Listen to Emily and Josh. **A:** Check (✓) Emily's likes in the chart. **B:** Check (✓) Josh's likes. Check together, and listen again to confirm. Do you think they can go on vacation together?

> I think they really can't go on vacation together, because …

D 🧑 **Make it personal** Check (✓) the activities you like doing on vacation. Are you more similar to Emily or Josh? Why? Tell a partner.

> I love to swim, and I don't like camping, so I'm more similar to Emily.

⚠️ **Common mistakes**

He's similar ~~with~~ *to* you.

♪ *Dance the night away, Live your life and stay young on the floor.*

2 Reading 5.3

A ▶5.13 **Read the two vacation ads quickly and answer questions 1–3 for each. Listen to check.**

1 What country is the ad for?   2 What kind of vacation is it?   3 When can you go?

Tropical Trek

Our **back**packer bus tours offer something for everyone who enjoys ad**ven**ture.

What to do: Swim, snorkel, scuba dive, kayak, visit an**c**ient Mayan **py**ramids, hike through a **fantastic rainforest**, search for **cro**codiles, **camp in the jun**gle.

Don't miss the spec**tac**ular **sun**rises, the howler m**on**keys, and the fla**min**gos!

Don't forget to lie in a **relaxing hammock** under a tree and spend some time doing nothing.

When to go: Mexico is a year-round destin**a**tion and the fun never stops.

YOGA RICA

Dis**co**ver our **yoga retreats** offered by local and international yoga pro**fe**ssionals.

What to do: take a yoga class, **me**ditate, have a massage, relax and read, walk in the **fo**rest, drink **her**bal tea.

Don't miss our guided tours to an **ac**tive volcano, **wonderful waterfalls**, rivers, **mou**ntains, and **beautiful beaches**.

Don't forget to finish your day with a **gour**met vege**tar**ian meal in our restaurant.

When to go: we offer retreats all year round in Costa Rica.

B Read the rule, then answer the questions.

Use *more* + adjective to form the comparative.

Which vacation in A:

1 is more active?   3 has more va**ri**ety?   5 is more dangerous?
2 is more relaxing?   4 is more healthy?   6 is more ad**ven**turous?

C ▶5.14 Match the **highlighted** words and phrases in the ads to photos 1–9. Listen, check, and repeat them. Which of the words with pink syllables are similar to your language?

D Which vacation do you prefer? Why?

I prefer the yoga retreat because I love relaxing on vacation, and I don't like hiking!

⚠ **Common mistakes**

taking
I enjoy ~~to take~~ selfies.

E 🎤 **Make it personal** In groups, design the perfect vacation. Decide:

a what type of vacation?   d how long?
b when?   e what activities?
c where?

5.4 How often do you leave voice messages?

1 Listening

House sitters
Young, active, professional couple looking to house sit in downtown area before buying. No kids, no pets. We totally understand the importance of loving your home. References provided.

A ▶5.15 Read the ad and guess True (T) or False (F). Listen to / Watch the video to check.

A house sitter is someone who:
1. usually pays to stay in a house.
2. lives in a house all the time.
3. cleans and cooks for the owner.
4. often takes care of pets.
5. leaves when the owner comes back.

B **Make it personal** In pairs, think of two advantages and disadvantages of being a house sitter. Would you like 1) to be or 2) to have a house sitter? Why (not)?

One advantage is that you can see if you like the area.

A disadvantage is that you have to leave when the owners return.

2 Vocabulary House sitting

A ▶5.16 Match the phrases to a–h in the picture. Listen, check, and repeat. Mime a phrase for a partner to say.

- [d] feed the cats / dog ___
- [ ] give the cats / dog some water ___
- [ ] turn on / off the lights ___
- [ ] walk the dog ___
- [ ] open / close the windows ___
- [ ] pick up / put the mail on the table ___
- [ ] water the plants ___
- [ ] don't let the cats out ___

B ▶5.17 Listen to a phone message for a house sitter. Number the activities in **A** in the order you hear them, 1–8.

♪ *Hey Jude, don't take it bad, take a sad song, and make it better. Remember to let it into your heart, then you can start to make it better.*

5.4

C ▶5.17 Listen again and complete Lori's notes with these pronouns. What does each pronoun refer to?

him   it   me   them (x 4)   us

1- Open the windows and close _____ again every day.
2- Pick up the mail, and put _____ on the table.
3- Feed the animals in the morning and evening (don't give _____ too much food).
4- The lights and air-conditioning - turn _____ off when you go out.
5- Don't forget to give _____ some water.
6- Walk Chips in the morning and afternoon (don't take _____ near the road).
7- Call _____ if you have any questions.
8- Please tell _____ if Salt, Pepper, or Chips escape.

→ **Grammar 5C** p. 146

D 👤 **Make it personal** Which is the most important thing to do when you house sit? Which is the least important? Compare in groups.

I think it's most important to feed the animals.

I think it's more important to give them water.

⏵ **Common mistakes**

Which is the ~~thing most important~~ *most important thing*?
The ~~less~~ *least* important thing is to put it on the table.

③ Grammar Imperatives

A Listen and read Lori's instructions in **2C** again and circle the correct options in the grammar box.

> Imperative verb forms:
> 1 **have** / **don't have** a subject.
> 2 use **don't** / **doesn't** for negative forms.
> 3 **are statements of fact** / **tell you to do something**.
> 4 go **up** ↗ / **down** ↘ at the end.

→ **Grammar 5D** p. 146

B In pairs, make ten instructions combining the words. Try them out with another pair. Use *please* to sound more polite.

open / close   your book / eyes
pick up / put down   your phone / pen
turn on / off   the lights / the air conditioning
point to   the teacher / the door

Please close the door. Don't open it again!

C 👤 **Make it personal** Imagine you're going on vacation.
1 Complete this list of instructions for a house sitter. Compare in groups. Who has the most useful instructions?
   1 Don't forget to _____.
   2 Please _____.
   3 Please don't _____.
   4 Remember to _____
   5 _____

Please don't have a party!

2 Leave a phone message for the house sitter. Use AS 5.17 on p. 163 to help you.

65

5.5 What's a staycation?

Skills Understanding instructions

A ▶5.18 Listen to the pairs of opposite adjectives and match them to pictures a–d. In pairs, can you think of others?
1. boring – fun / interesting
2. expensive – cheap
3. safe – dangerous
4. neat – messy

How about rude and polite?

B ▶5.19 Listen, and read about two alternative types of vacations, 1 and 2. Match them to their best definition. There's one extra.
- ☐ You take a vacation at home.
- ☐ You go and stay in another person's home.
- ☐ You pay to stay in someone's home.

Vacations for less!

1 Couchsurfing helps you stay free in about 200,000 cities around the world. Couchsurfing.org is an international network and there are more than 12 million members. Members offer people a place to stay in their homes. In return, they can stay free at another member's home. Members are students and professionals. You can be a surfer or a host or both!

If you want to couchsurf, here's what to do:
- Find a host who has positive references and a complete profile.
- Look for a host who has similar interests.
- Write a request to your potential host.
- Be a good guest.
- Don't be rude or messy! Help with the household chores.
- Write a reference as soon as possible to help other couchsurfers.

2 A **staycation** is a vacation that you spend at home! It's a way to have a rest from work and your routine without spending much money. Maybe it sounds boring, but it doesn't have to be.

Here are some tips to make your staycation fun:
- Spend time at home. Invite friends to use your pool or have dinner.
- Visit local parks and museums. There are often really cool things in your hometown.
- Find out about local festivals in your area.
- Change your routine – don't do what you usually do every day. Do something different. Get up late. Change stores. Eat different foods. Take a bus, ride a bike, or walk for a change.
- Relax and don't think about work until your staycation is over.

C Read again and write True (T) or False (F).
1. Couchsurfing only happens in Europe.
2. You don't pay to couchsurf.
3. Couchsurfers write references and requests.
4. Staycations are for boring people.
5. People on staycation don't go out.
6. On a staycation, the idea is to do different things.

D ▶5.20 Listen to six sentences from the text and say *staycation* or *couchsurfing* after each.

E 🔴 Make it personal In pairs. Write five instructions for:
a) a couchsurfer visiting your town OR
b) a person who wants to staycation in your hometown.

Compare instructions with another pair. Do you agree with theirs?

Our first instruction for a couchsurfer is: Don't make noise.   *That's a good one. That's very important.*

For a staycation in our hometown: Visit the market.

66

5.5 Do you live near here?

♪ *In my place, in my place. Were lines that I couldn't change, And I was lost, oh yeah, I was lost.*

 in Action Giving directions

A ▶5.21 Match the phrases to photos 1–6. Listen, repeat, and mime them.

- [ ] a corner
- [ ] cross at the stoplight
- [1] go straight
- [ ] a stop sign
- [ ] turn left
- [ ] turn right

B In pairs, share what you know about San Francisco in one minute.

I know it's a large city on the west coast of the U.S.

Common mistakes

Do you know where ~~is~~ the stadium?   is

Turn ~~to~~ left.

C ▶5.22 Listen to and order the tourist's questions, 1–4. How many people does he speak to?
- [ ] Is there a movie theater around here?
- [ ] Are there any bookstores near here?
- [ ] Where's the mall?
- [ ] Do you know where the library is?

D ▶5.22 Listen again and complete 1–4. Do you think he understands the last man?

1 It's _____ front of you _____ Market Street. Cross _____ at the stoplight.
2 Go _____ on Market Street and turn _____ on Fourth Street. Go _____ for one block, and the movie theater's on the _____ of Fourth and Mission Street.
3 Turn _____ on Grove Street.
4 Go straight for about _____ blocks. The bookstore's on your _____.

E In pairs, use the language above to ask for and give directions to places 1–4. Start at Powell Street Station.
1 City Hall
2 the Museum of Modern Art
3 Union Square Park
4 a parking garage

F **Make it personal** In pairs. **A:** Give directions to your home from school. **B:** Follow the directions on a map until you find where **A** lives.

Leave the school and turn left. Go straight for two blocks. My house is on the left.

Writing 5   A city brochure

Round my hometown, Memories are fresh, Round my hometown, Ooh the people I've met, Are the wonders of my world.

A What do you know about Vancouver? Say what you see in the photos.

B Read the brochure entry and answer questions 1–8.
1. Where's a good place to start the day?
2. Where's a beautiful place for photos?
3. What's a good place to go when it's rainy?
4. What's a good place to go to buy souvenirs?
5. What are three examples of places to eat lunch?
6. Is there a romantic place in this city?
7. What can tourists do at night?
8. Is this city famous for anything?

A DAY IN VANCOUVER

- Welcome to Canada's third – but most beautiful – city! First, have breakfast at Purebread Bakery in Gastown. The coffee and chocolate brownies <u>are delicious</u>!
- After eating, rent a bike and ride to Stanley Park. This is an <u>enormous park</u> downtown with lots of monuments, live concerts, street artists, and wildlife. There are <u>beautiful views</u> of the mountains. Before leaving, visit Prospect Point and take some photos of the ocean.
- After that, take the subway to the Museum of Vancouver. Vancouver is famous for its First Nations art, and you can see some amazing <u>old and modern art,</u> and <u>cultural objects</u>.
- When you leave the museum, go back downtown. There are hundreds of restaurants for lunch: Asian noodle restaurants, Canadian seafood cafés with <u>fresh fish</u>, and lots of great American burger bars. Go to Main Street after lunch and shop in the local <u>independent stores</u>, then take a water taxi to the public market at Granville Island.
- Finally, Vancouver has great nightlife, with many clubs and music venues. And you have to visit the Top of Vancouver revolving restaurant for a night-time view of this incredible city – <u>it's very romantic</u>.

C Study the underlined words in **B** and answer 1–3.
1. Do adjectives come before or after a noun?
2. Do adjectives come before or after the verb *be*?
3. Can you make adjectives plural?

D Order the words to make sentences.
1. is / wine / for / France / famous / .
2. the / try / cheese / local / .
3. spectacular / a / there / view / is / .
4. mountains / can / in / beautiful / the / walk / you / .
5. visit / amazing / can / you / museum / the / .

E Read **Write it right!** and find eight sequencing words in **B**.

✓ Write it right!

Use sequencing words to order actions: *before, after, when, first, then, finally,* etc.
You can take photos in the park. **After that**, go to the museum.
After taking (or **After** you take) photos, go to the museum.
Before going (or **Before** you go) to the museum, take some photos in the park.

F Note your answers to 1–8 in **B** for your town or city.

G **Make it personal** Imagine a tourist is coming to your town / city. Plan a day for her / him.

Before	Use your notes for **F**. Give extra information, too, e.g., your opinion.
While	Use adjectives and a variety of sequencing words.
After	Check your writing carefully and / or email it to a partner before giving it to your teacher.

5 Miss GPS

1 Before watching

A Match the nouns with the verb phrases to make sentences.
1 A map   gets you from one place to another.
2 A car   picks up a signal so you can make a call.
3 GPS / sat nav   always shows you where north is.
4 A compass   shows roads and highways.
5 A cell phone   can give you directions by voice.

B Number the items 1–8 in your order of importance for a road trip to a new place.
a car / motorbike ☐   a phone charger ☐
a cell phone ☐   food and drink ☐
a map ☐   good company ☐
extra batteries ☐   music you enjoy ☐

C ⬤ Make it personal Compare and explain in pairs. Many differences?

> I hate maps, so for me that's number 8. My number 1 is good company!

> I'm different. I like to travel alone, so my number 1 is music I enjoy.

D In pairs, choose four items from A and B you think the actors use on their trip. Watch to check. Were you right?

2 While watching

A Complete 1–12 with the correct form of the verbs. Who says them?

| avoid | hate | have | go | like | love (x 2) |
| save | take | tell | use | waste | |

1 Does anyone _____ a map?
2 Maps? Who _____ maps anymore?
3 I _____ using maps. Especially old maps.
4 Here she is. Miss GPS. You _____?
5 We don't _____ anywhere without GPS, right Auggie?
6 Technology _____ all the fun out of traveling.
7 I disagree. Technology _____ time.
8 And it _____ us where we're going, while we're driving.
9 Come on. Let's not _____ time arguing.
10 And a GPS helps us _____ traffic. A map can't do that.
11 And I _____ hearing the sound of my GPS girl's voice.
12 I _____ hearing that voice. It's so annoying!

B ⬤ Make it personal In pairs, talk about technology. Which items do you love? Any you find annoying?

> I love electricity. Without it, I can't do anything!

> I love cell phones, but sometimes ring tones are annoying.

3 After watching

A What happens on the trip? Write True (T) or False (F). Correct the false sentences.
1 They get lost.
2 Daniel forgets to plug in the GPS.
3 The GPS battery's dead.
4 August has a strong signal on his cell phone.
5 They stop the car and ask for directions.
6 Andrea uses a map and gives directions.
7 August gets a signal on his cell phone.

B Who says it? Match 1–8 to Andrea (An), August (A), Daniel (D), Lucy (L). Watch again and imitate the actors.

	An	A	D	L
1 GPS! Not always reliable.				
2 Are you kidding me?				
3 Not a car in sight and no signal. We are so lost.				
4 Especially when you forget to plug it in.				
5 I'm gonna get a signal, don't worry.				
6 What are we gonna do? Turn back?				
7 Lucy and I will give directions from now on.				
8 After that, we're back on the main road.				

C ⬤ Make it personal Which do you prefer? Compare in pairs. Why?
1 giving the driver directions or driving the car
2 driving or taking a taxi
3 driving in the city or in the country
4 walking or cycling
5 using a GPS with the voice on or off

> I like driving and I'm not good with maps. So, I prefer driving.

69

Mid-term review — Play *Thirty Seconds*.

- 4 to 8 players. Divide into 2 teams.
- From the start, teams go in opposite directions.
- Toss a coin.
   Heads move 1 square.
   Tails move 2 squares.
- Talk about the topic, answer the question, or do the activity on the square. Maximum 30 seconds per person.
- The winning team is the first to complete the full circuit.

Grammar Unit 1

1A Verb *be* ⊕ ⊖ and *Yes / No* ❓

The verb *be* only has three forms: *am, is, are*.
Use contractions when you speak or write informally.

⊕	Contractions	
I *am*	I'm	a student.
You (singular) *are*	You're	Latin American.
He / She / It *is*	He's / She's / It's	Panamanian.
We *are*	We're	from Brazil.
You (plural) *are*	You're	students.
They *are*	They're	British.

⊖	
I'm not	Colombian.
You're not or aren't	Asian.
He's / She's / It's not or isn't	Spanish.
We / You / They're not or aren't	Canadian.

	Short answers	
❓	Yes	No
Are you from the U.S.? Are you American?	Yes, I am. Yes, I'm Texan.	No, I'm not.
Is he a great player? Is she an OK actor? Is it a Chinese phone?	Yes, he is. Yes, she is. Yes, it is.	No, he's not. / isn't. No, she's not. / isn't. No, it is not. / isn't.
Are you students?	Yes, we are.	No, we're not. / aren't.
Are they actors?	Yes, they are.	No, they're not. / aren't.

We usually answer *Yes / No* questions with a short answer.
Are you Spanish? Yes, I am. NOT ~~Yes, I'm.~~
Do not use contractions with ⊕ short answers.

1B Adjectives and *a / an* + noun

a	an
She's **a** good person.	He's **an** interesting person.

Use **a** before a consonant sound / **an** before a vowel sound.

Adjectives

article adjective noun	article adjective noun
Neymar's a Brazilian soccer player.	Jennifer Lawrence is a fantastic actor.
Buenos Aires is a great city.	This is a green book. Those are green books.

In English, the adjective comes *before* a noun, and doesn't have a plural form.

1C Verb *be*: *Wh-* ❓

- What's your address?
- Where are you from?
- Why are they here?
- When's your birthday?
- Who's he?
- How are you?

Wh- question words come before the verb *be*.
Remember to invert in questions.
Where are you from? NOT ~~Where you are from?~~

1D Demonstrative pronouns

Use *this / these* for things or people that are with you or near you (here).
- **This** is my pen. (It's with me.)
- **These** are my keys. (They're here.)

Use *that / those* for things or people that are with other people or distant from you (there).
- **That**'s my pen. (It's on the table.)
- **Those** are my keys. (They're there.)

Remember to invert in questions.
Is this your book? NOT ~~This is your book?~~
Use pronouns in answers.
Yes, it is. NOT ~~Yes, this is.~~

1E Possessive adjectives

Subject pronoun	Possessive adjective
I	**My** car is blue.
You	**Your** green glasses are on the table.
He	**His** new laptop is fantastic.
She	That's **her** teacher.
It	This is my dog. Oh, what's **its** name?
We	**Our** friends are here.
You	Please turn off **your** cell phones.
They	**Their** city is really cool.

Possessive adjectives only have one form.
Possessive adjectives go before a noun or an adjective + noun.
My new shoes. NOT ~~Mys shoes news.~~

Hi, I'm your teacher. My name's Bruno.

Unit 1

1A

1 Complete 1–5 with verb *be*. Use contractions when possible.
1. He _____ not from the U.S. He _____ Canadian.
2. We _____ not Hawaiian, we _____ Mexican.
3. It _____ not an Irish flag, it _____ an Italian flag.
4. They _____ from NY, but the statue _____ from France!
5. Her name _____ not Emma. It _____ Emily.

2 Complete 1–5 with verb *be*. In pairs, ask and answer. Remember to use short answers when possible.
1. _____ you Chilean?
2. _____ Christ the Redeemer statue in Spain?
3. _____ Justin Bieber American?
4. _____ you and Neymar friends?
5. _____ Idris Elba and Emily Blunt British?

1B

1 Correct the mistakes.
1. She's a girl cool.
2. They're not actors terrible.
3. Rio de Janeiro is a city excellent.
4. You're a player fantastic.
5. Is it a car Korean?

2 Order the words to make sentences.
1. interesting / is / San Francisco / an / city / .
2. actor / intelligent / an / Antonio Banderas / is / .
3. players / are / they / important / soccer / .
4. is / a / ridiculous / it / movie / .
5. excellent / I / student / an / am / .

1C

1 Order the words to make *Wh-* questions.
1. the name of / what / in Mexico / 's / that place / ?
2. are / when / home / you / ?
3. who / your / 's / friend / best / ?
4. you / why / are / here / ?
5. email / 's / what / address / your / ?

2 Correct the mistakes.
1. How's her name?
2. What's your favorite actor?
3. Is where his laptop?
4. Why you're in this class?
5. What's your favorite cities?

1D

1 Look at the examples and write questions and answers.
What are those?   Those are ...
What's this?   This is ...

2 Complete with the correct demonstrative pronoun.
1. _____ is a blue bookbag.
2. Is _____ your friend Tina?
3. _____ are my friends, Dan and Mary.
4. _____ is not my homework. _____ is my homework.
5. _____ is my email address.

1E

1 Correct two mistakes in each.
1. Her name is José and she's from Spain.
2. I think his name is Mary. She's american.
3. Is we in the same English class?
4. These is our teacher, Ms. Jones. We are in his class.
5. That not my phone. The my phone is black.

2 Complete with the correct possessive adjectives.
1. _____ name is Daniel and I'm from Mexico.
2. This is my friend. _____ name is Karina.
3. We are in English class together. _____ school is in California.
4. This is our new teacher. _____ name is Bruno.
5. These are my parents. _____ names are David and Marcia.

Grammar Unit 2

2A Simple present ⊕ ⊖

The simple present only has two forms:
1 The infinitive, used for *I / You / We / They*
2 The infinitive + *s* used for *He / She / It*

Use the simple present:
– for routines, habits, repeated actions
– for facts
– for scheduled events
– with time phrases (*every morning, sometimes*, etc.)

▸ *I wake up at 7 a.m. every day.* (routine)
▸ *You never study before tests.* (habit)
▸ *Banks don't open on weekends.* (fact)
▸ *We have a meeting today at 2 p.m.* (scheduled event)

Subject	⊕	
I / You / We / They	live	in Paris.

Subject	⊖	
I / You / We / They	do not / don't live	in Ecuador.

⊕ Use *I, you, we,* and *they* + the infinitive. (I)
⊖ Use *do* + *not* before the verb. Contraction = *don't*.
We don't have a car. NOT *We have no car.*

Third person singular: *she, he,* and *it* + *s*

Subject	⊕	
She / He	plays	volleyball.

Subject	⊖	
She / He	doesn't play	golf.

Spelling rules:
Most verbs add *-s*: *knows, speaks, loves*.
Verbs ending in *-ch, -sh, -ss, -x*, or *-o*, add *-es*: *ch – watches; sh – finishes; ss – kisses; x – mixes; o – goes*.
Verbs ending in consonant + *-y*: change *y* to *i* and add *-es*: *study – studies*.

Notes:
do ends with *o*, so it is spelled *-es* (*does*) in the third person.
When we use the auxiliary, the main verb is always an infinitive:
▸ *He works here. – He doesn't work here.*
▸ *She goes to school. – She doesn't go to school*

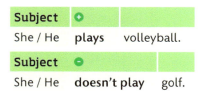
Why does Superman have an ?
Because he is the ***third person***.
*He hate**s** kryptonite, he love**s** Lois, and he do**es**n't like bad guys!*

2B Simple present ❓

A	S	I (O)	Short answers
Do	you	**like** sports?	Yes, I do. / No, I don't.
Does	he	**live** here?	Yes, he does. / No, he doesn't.
Does	she	**play** tennis?	Yes, she does. / No, she doesn't.
Do	they	**work** near here?	Yes, they do. / No, they don't.

To form a *Yes / No* question use:
Auxiliary (*do / does*) + Subject + Infinitive (+ object) = **A S I (O)**.
Short answers use: *do / does* or *don't / doesn't*.

Q	A	S	I (O)
When	do	you	get up?
What	does	Joe	do in the evenings?
Why	does	Sue	work at night?
How	do	they	go to the beach?

To form a *Wh-* question use:
Question word + Auxiliary (*do / does*) + Subject + Infinitive (+ object) = **Q A S I (O)**.

2C Frequency adverbs

100% → **always** → **usually** → **often** → **sometimes** → **occasionally** → **rarely** → **never** → 0%

▸ How **often** do you drink coffee?
 I **always** have two cups for breakfast.
▸ How **often** does he exercise?
 He **rarely** exercises.

Adverbs of frequency go before the main verb.

Use **time expressions** to say how many times something occurs.

▸ When do you go to the gym?
 I go to the gym at 7 a.m. on Mondays and Wednesdays.
 = I go to the gym **twice a week**.
▸ I go out every Saturday. = I go out **once a week**.

2D Prepositions of time

▸ *I sometimes go to work **at** around 5:15 p.m.*
▸ *We never go out **at** night.*
▸ *Dad usually visits me **at** Christmas.*

Use *at* with times, night, and holidays (without day).

▸ *Our vacation is always **in** January.*
▸ *See you **in** the morning / afternoon / evening.*

Use *in* with months and parts of a day (except *night*).

▸ *I do yoga **on** Tuesdays / Tuesday nights.*
▸ *I rarely work **on** Friday (evenings).*
▸ *We go shopping **on** weekends.*

Use *on* with days, day + part of a day, and *weekend*.

Unit 2

2A

1 Match the verbs to the people. Then complete 1–6.

drive   exercise   have breakfast
leave home   live   walk

1 Jane _____ at 8 a.m.
2 Mr. Jones _____ to work every day.
3 Andy _____ Jane to school by 8:30.
4 Mary and Jack _____ at 8 a.m.
5 Miguel _____ in the morning.
6 They all _____ in houses.

2 Make negative sentences about the people in 1.

1 Miguel _____ 8 a.m. (**not leave home**)
2 Jane _____ on weekdays. (**not exercise**)
3 Andy and Jane _____ at 8 a.m. (**not have breakfast**)
4 Mary and Jack _____ to work. (**not walk**)
5 Mr. Jones _____ to work every day. (**not drive**)
6 Mary _____ with Andy. (**not live**)

3 Circle the correct auxiliary.

1 What time **do** / **does** they usually get up?
2 When **do** / **does** he leave for work in the morning?
3 **Do** / **Does** you live with your parents?
4 Where **do** / **does** people go shopping in this neighborhood?
5 **Don't** / **Doesn't** we have school in December?
6 Where **do** / **does** their dog live?

2B

1 Order the words to make *Wh-* questions.

1 have / breakfast / you / do / when / ?
2 go / where / he / morning / does / every / ?
3 out / usually / time / what / she / does / go / ?
4 at / they / gym / often / exercise / the / how / do / ?
5 who / visit / when / go / you / do / you / Texas / to / ?

2 Complete the dialogue with auxiliaries.

A: Wow, you're here! _____ you always come to class this early?
B: No. I _____ always get here this early on Mondays.
A: I see. Well, _____ the class always start on time?
B: Hmm, sometimes it _____, but occasionally it _____. We never know.
A: Hey, _____ that girl always sit at the back of the class?
B: Yes, she _____. And she always listens to music before class.
A: I _____ that, too.

2C

1 Match the frequency adverbs to sentences 1–5.

1 They study on Mondays, Tuesdays, Fridays, and Sundays.
2 She goes to the office on Tuesdays and Thursdays.
3 He likes to relax and play video games every day.
4 They don't travel together.
5 We visit our parents twice a year.

☐ never   ☐ always   ☐ often
☐ rarely   ☐ sometimes

2D

1 Circle the correct preposition.

1 We are always in class **at** / **in** / **on** 3 p.m.
2 Jackie is never **at** / **in** / **on** time for work.
3 You can complete this language course **at** / **in** / **on** 15 hours.
4 His birthday is **at** / **in** / **on** Monday. Let's have a party!
5 They start the semester **at** / **in** / **on** January.

Grammar Unit 3

3A Present continuous ➕ ➖

Subject	Present of *be*	Verb + *ing* + object	
I	am / am not 'm / 'm not	reading	this box.
You / We / They	are / are not 're not / aren't		
She / He / It	is / is not 's not / isn't	walking	right now.

Use the **present continuous** for actions in progress now.
Do not contract **am** + **not** (~~I amn't~~).

Spelling

Present participle (-*ing*)	Spelling rule
She's **listening** to a song. They're **playing** a game.	Most verbs, add -*ing*.
I'm **making** a cake. Our train's **arriving**.	Verbs ending in -*e*, change -*e* to -*ing*.
They're **running** a race. I'm **sitting** alone.	Verbs ending in consonant + vowel + consonant (CVC), double the final C + -*ing*.
Look! Mike's **boxing** now.	Don't double consonants *x* or *w*.

3B Present continuous ❓

Yes / No ❓

Present of *be*	Subject	Verb + *ing* + object	
Am	I	listening	to the news?
Are / Aren't	you / we / they		
Is / Isn't	she / he		
Is / Isn't	it	raining	now?

We usually answer *Yes / No* questions with a short answer.
▸ *Aren't you coming with me?* *Yes, I am. / No, I'm not.*

Wh- ❓

Wh- word	Present of *be*	Subject	Verb + *ing* + object	
Who	am	I	talking	to?
Why	are	you / we / they	driving	fast?
When	is	she / he	running	that marathon?
Where	is	it	raining	now?

We often use contractions in questions and responses.
▸ *What's she doing?*
She's watching the weather report.

Present continuous for things happening around now

At the moment	Around now
I'm watching TV right now.	I'm watching TV a lot these days.
Look! He's taking her money!	I'm taking dance lessons this semester.

It is very common to use the **present continuous** to talk about things that are happening around now.

3C Simple present and present continuous

Use the **simple present** for a daily habit, routine, facts, or scheduled events.

Use the **present continuous** for:
▸ an action happening at the moment or a break in a routine.
▸ processes in progress but not necessarily happening right now.
I'm doing a degree in Engineering (but I'm not studying today).
▸ for future plans/arrangements. (see Unit 9)
What are you doing after class?
I'm going home, then I'm working. NOT ~~I go home then I work.~~
Are you coming out later?
No, we're staying home all weekend.

Other future time expressions; *in a few minutes, this evening, tonight, tomorrow (morning), next week, this semester, in the summer,* etc. (See Unit 9)

Routine / Habit	Now, developing, or breaking routine
It never snows in March.	Look, it's snowing! (now)
I go to the salon every Saturday.	I'm driving to the salon. (now)

Adverbs of frequency and time phrases can help you decide when to use **simple present** or **present continuous**.

Simple present	Present continuous
always, sometimes, usually, often, every day, occasionally, never, first, next, then, rarely	at the moment, at this moment, just, right now, just now, now, still

Verbs for emotion, senses, or mental states

adore, appear, be, believe, dislike, hate, have, know, like, look, love, mean, prefer, remember, see, seem, smell, sound, surprise, understand, want.

Use the **simple present** not the present continuous with these verbs.

Correct	Incorrect
He believes you.	He's believing you.
She doesn't understand.	She's not understanding.
They like this party.	They're liking this party.
Do you remember it all?	Are you remembering it all?

Note: Phrases like "I'm loving it!" or "I'm liking this." are now used in informal conversation.

Unit 3

3A

1 Complete 1–6 with the present continuous.
1 Look, it _____ today. But it's really windy. (**not / rain**)
2 Why _____ her homework? (**not / do**)
3 Are you _____ a friend and _____ to me at the same time? (**text**) (**talk**)
4 Excuse me, I _____ the subway station. (**look for**)
5 Where _____ the other students _____ after class? (**go**)
6 I think they _____ for a coffee. (**meet**)

2 Look at the example and write sentences about the picture.

Victor is sleeping.

3B

1 Order 1–6 to form questions, then ask and answer in pairs.
1 right now / what / you / doing / are / ?
2 you / are / at the moment / with your family / living / ?
3 doing / much exercise / you / these days / are / ?
4 working / at the moment / where / are / you / ?
5 another / Chinese / are / or / studying / you / language / ?
6 learning / you / why / are / English / here / ?

2 Do 1–7 refer to right now (RN), around now (AN), or future (F)?
1 I'm watching a great show on TV, so I can't chat.
2 We're watching a lot of TV at the moment, usually around three hours a day!
3 I'm not coming on Monday, I'm going to the dentist's.
4 I'm working in Paris at the moment, lucky me!
5 I'm still working, so I can't come to the movies with you.
6 The sun is shining and we're sitting on the beach.
7 We're leaving early tonight to avoid the traffic.

3C

1 Correct the mistakes.
1 Hey. What do you do? Are you busy?
   No. I have lunch right now. What do you think of doing?
2 Where is she buying her clothes? I am wanting to go there, too!
   Yeah! She looking great. I think about buying the same dress!
3 Hey, where does he go? We having a meeting in a few minutes.
   I am not knowing. He talk on his cell phone in the hall.
4 I'm not believing you all finally here. Wow!
   Yeah, and we stay at a great hotel! We love New York in the summer.
5 I'm have a salad. Are you just eat a hamburger?
   No, I'm not. I'm always ordering French fries and a soda.

2 Circle the correct form of the verb.
1 I **'m talking / talk** to you on the phone and walking.
2 We often **are cooking / cook** dinner before watching TV.
3 I **'m hating / hate** talking about politics in class.
4 She **'s riding / rides** a bike to work, because her car is at the mechanic's.
5 He's not at the office, so he **emails / 's emailing** us from his smartphone.
6 I **'m not going / don't go** out tonight. I'm too tired.

143

Grammar Unit 4

4A Definite article *the*

English has only one definite article: *the*. The form never changes.
Use *the*
- to refer to something already mentioned.
  *I rent a place here. **The** apartment's very nice.*
- when you imagine there's only one.
  *Where's **the** bathroom?*
- before superlatives and ordinal numbers.
  *"Uptown Funk" is **the** best Bruno Mars song.*
  *These are **the** first mangoes of the year.*

Do not use *the*
- with plural nouns.
  I love beans.
- with uncountable nouns.
  We often eat rice.
- to talk about things in general.
  I don't like politics, I enjoy watching detective movies.

4B *Can*

Can: ➕ ➖

Subject	Modal	Infinitive (+ object)
I / You	can	play the piano.
He / She / It	can't /	drive a truck.
We / They	cannot	speak English.
		dance well.

Can is a modal auxiliary verb with the same form for all persons. It is followed by infinitive without *to*.
We can swim. NOT *We can to swim.*
It means "be able to" or "know how to":
- *I **can** play tennis. = I'm able to play tennis.*
- *I **can't** drive = I don't know how to drive.*

Use *well*, *very well*, *(not) at all* to describe the level of ability.
- *He **can't** ride a bike **very well**, but he **can** run.*
- *We **can't** play the piano **at all**, but we **can** sing **well**!*
- *She **can't** play golf, but she **can** play soccer **very well**.*

Can: Yes / No ❓

Modal	Subject	Infinitive (+ object)	Short answers
Can / Can't	I / you / she / he / we / they	sing? come to the party? ski?	Yes, ___ can. / No, ___ can't.

- *I **can** speak English, but I **can't** speak Japanese.*

Can: Wh- ❓

Q	A modal (*can*)	S	I (+ object)
What	can	you	play on the piano?

Other meanings of *can*

Can has many different uses. Here are a few:
- **Possibility**: *You can read about the school on their website.*
- **Requests**: *Can I please see your passport and ID?*
- **Permission**: *You can use my car, but you have to come home by 10 p.m.*
- **Favors**: *Please can you pick me up at the airport?*

4C Possessive pronouns

Possessive adjective	Possessive pronoun
This is not **my** jacket.	**Mine**'s blue.
I think **your** keys are on the table.	These keys aren't **yours**.
Are those **his** glasses?	No, these green glasses are **his**.
Is that **her** phone?	No, this white phone is **hers**.
These are **our** sandwiches.	But those cookies aren't **ours**.
I think **your** coats are over there.	Are they **yours**?
Their house is beautiful.	Which house is **theirs**?

English only has six possessive pronouns. *Yours* is both singular and plural. A **possessive pronoun** substitutes a possessive adjective + noun.
Use ***Whose*** to ask about possession.
- *Whose book is that? Whose books are those?*

NOT *Of who is this book?*

4D Possessive *'s*

1. Add *'s* to names and nouns to indicate possession.
   That's the teacher's chair. NOT *That's the chair of the teacher.*
   - *That book is Jenna's.* → *It's hers.*
   - *Isn't that Nina's car?*
   - *This is someone's money, but not mine.*

2. Names ending in *-s*, use *'s* or just an apostrophe after the letter (*s'*).
   - *It's James's iPad. = It's James' iPad.*

3. Regular plurals add an apostrophe after the *s*.
   - *Isn't that your parents' house?*

4. Irregular plurals add *'s*.
   - *Which are your children's toys?*

144

Unit 4

4A

1 Circle the correct article in 1–10 (θ = no article).
1. I love **a / the / θ** dogs, but I hate **a / the / θ** cats.
2. We live in **a / the / θ** small house. My grandmother lives on **a / the / θ** same street.
3. Excuse me. Can you tell me where **an / the / θ** elevator is?
4. I need **a / the / θ** chocolate! Where's **a / the / θ** nearest grocery store?
5. My brother lives on **a / the / θ** first floor of that building. It's **a / the / θ** great apartment.
6. I never eat **a / the / θ** French fries at **a / the / θ** home.
7. **a / the / θ** Camila's sister has **a / the / θ** green eyes and **a / the / θ** beautiful dark hair.
8. I love **a / the / θ** sports and I'm really enjoying **a / the / θ** sports documentary series on Channel 5.
9. I never eat **a / the / θ** breakfast on **a / the / θ** weekends.
10. I hate **a / the / θ** messy people!

4B

1 Complete 1–5 with *can / can't* and the verbs.

drive   play   ride   swim   use

1. He loves American football. He _____ very well.
2. Is that your new bike? _____ you _____ it? It looks too big!
3. This hotel has an amazing pool. It's too bad I _____.
4. I don't know how she's a writer. She _____ a computer!
5. _____ you _____? I need to get home quickly!

2 What can / can't each person in the pictures do? Use your own ideas.
1. Lee can _____, but he can't _____.
2. Martin can't _____, but he can _____.
3. George can't _____, but he can _____.
4. Janice can _____, but she can't _____.
5. May can't _____, but she can _____.

3 Write *Wh-* questions for answers 1–5.
1. We can be at the train station by 6 o'clock.
   What time can you be at the train station?
2. You can take the train from Central Station.
3. He can't play soccer or baseball.
4. My mother can cook Italian food really well!
5. We can serve your breakfast from 7 to 10 a.m.

4 Are 1–5 ability (A), possibility (P), or request (R)?
1. Can you come to a party on Saturday night? _____
2. Can we open the window, please? _____
3. Can't we get tickets for the movie tonight? _____
4. Can I use your car this weekend? _____
5. Can she play the piano and sing? _____
6. Can you watch my bike for a moment, please? _____
7. Can you read that page without your glasses? _____
8. Can you help me with my homework, please? _____
9. Can you tell me how to get to Fifth Street? _____
10. Can you explain that word, please? _____

4C

1 Complete 1–5 with a possessive pronoun.
1. I'm a musician. That guitar is _____.
2. Marcy is always talking to somebody! I think that phone is _____.
3. Your sneakers are blue, not red. Are you sure these are _____?
4. It's really cold in here. Are those _____ sweaters?
5. It looks like Joe's wallet, but I don't think it's _____. He's traveling.

4D

1 Add the possessives ('s) or (').
1. Those are not my shoes, those are Marcus.
2. Where is your grandparent house?
3. My sisters new pants are yellow and blue.
4. That is Charles desk. His dad office is over there.
5. Her friends phone numbers are in her contact list.
6. My mom favorite album is *Queen Greatest Hits*.

145

Grammar Unit 5

5A *There is / are* ⊕ ⊖ ❓

There is / are ⊕ ⊖

	⊕	⊖	
Singular	There is a park near the river.	There's no / There isn't a	mall near here.
Plural	There are 20 people in the room.	There are no / There aren't any	animals in there.

Use *there is / are* to express "existence" in a physical space.
For negatives, use *there 's / is / are* + *no* or *there isn't / aren't* + *a / any*.

There is / are ❓

❓			Short answers
Is		a bank near here? an answer to the question?	Yes, there is. No, there isn't.
Are	there	any tourists here? any good restaurants in this area?	Yes, there are. No, there aren't.
Isn't		a swimming pool around here?	Yes, there is. No, there isn't.
Aren't		any cups on the table?	Yes, there are. No, there aren't.

Do not use contractions in ⊕ short answers.
Yes, there is. NOT *Yes, there's.*

5B *like / love / hate / enjoy / not mind* + verb *-ing*

I	love	to swim / swimming
You	like	to camp / camping
Tom	likes	to read / reading novels.
Nina	doesn't mind	waking up early.
We	hate	cleaning the house.
You	enjoy	listening to music
My brothers	hate	playing baseball.

I don't mind going out on weekends. NOT *I don't mind to go out…*

Note: Use the gerund (verb + *-ing* which functions as a noun) as the subject of a sentence.
- *Swimming is my favorite sport.*
- *Playing tennis is awesome.*
- *Studying on the weekend is boring!*

Speaking English is important. NOT *To speak English is important.*

5C Object pronouns

Subject	Object
I love animals, but I don't think they like	**me**.
You're always trying to help. But who's helping	**you**?
Martin says people don't understand	**him**.
Marta's not coming. But why don't you call	**her**?
Your bag's on the floor. Please put	**it** on a chair.
Don't worry, **we**'re OK. Everything's fine with	**us**.
The windows are open, can you close	**them**, please?

English only has seven object pronouns. Use an **object pronoun** to substitute the **object** of the sentence.
It and *you* (singular and plural) have the same form for both subject and object pronouns.
The other five have different forms.
The object pronoun comes after the verb.
She loves him but he doesn't love her. NOT *She him loves but he doesn't her love.*

Note: We usually refer to an animal with a name as **he / him** or **she / her**.
- *Our dog, Bart, is great. He's really friendly! We all adore him.*

5D Imperatives ⊕ and ⊖

⊕	⊖
Sit down.	Don't sit down.
Stand up.	Don't stand up.

Use **imperatives** to give orders or make requests.
- *Go away!* (order)
- *Don't touch that!* (order)

Imperatives only have one form for all persons.
Use *please* to make a request and sound polite.
- *Please be quiet.*
- *Don't talk here, please.*

There is no subject in an imperative sentence.
Don't go! NOT *Don't you go!*

5E Comparatives and superlatives

To form comparatives and superlatives with long adjectives use
more / less + **the most / the least** + adjective
- *You're more adventurous than me.*
- *I'm less intelligent than you.*
- *Joao's the most adventurous in our class.*
- *Who's the least intelligent?*

See p. 156 for more rules.

Unit 5

5A

1 Complete 1–5 with verb *be*. Contract when possible.
1. There _____ a racetrack in Belmont, Long Island.
2. There _____ very important horse races at the track.
3. We're happy because there _____ a new movie theater near us.
4. There _____ three nice hotels and two museums in this city.
5. In our city, there _____ a famous monument next to the station.

2 Order 1–6 to make sentences. Then change them so they're true for you.
1. city / is / football / there / an / enormous / stadium / my / in / .
2. this / restaurants / neighborhood / any / around / aren't / there / .
3. exhibition / is / good / our / local / museum / a / at / there / art / .
4. in / mall / no / there / is / neighborhood / this / .
5. street / my / there / swimming / a / on / isn't / pool / .
6. in / river / a / middle / city / of / our / clean / 's / the / there / capital / .

5B

1 Circle the correct alternative.
1. My son really loves **reading / read** comic books.
2. My little sister doesn't mind **to take / taking** piano lessons twice a week.
3. All our friends love **playing / play** and enjoy **watch / watching** international soccer.
4. I really like **go / going** to the movies, but it's expensive.
5. We hate **shop / shopping** and **to doing / doing** the laundry.

2 Correct two mistakes in each.
1. Anna loves wash dishes and to clean the bathroom.
2. I hate to reading novels. I like read biographies or true stories.
3. He doesn't mind to see a romantic movie sometimes, but he not enjoy horror movies.
4. We love to eating out on the weekend. We doesn't like cooking at home.
5. They hate to doing laundry, but don't mind to do dishes.
6. On vacation, I enjoy to hiking and snorkel, but I never go kayaking.

5C

1 Circle the correct object pronouns.
1. Ranger Juan works at this station. Please respect **him / her / it**.
2. There are bears in the park. Please don't feed **it / them / us**.
3. Cars are not allowed. Leave **their / they / them** in the parking lot.
4. Don't leave garbage at the campsite. Throw **him / her / it** in the trash.
5. We're here to help. Tell **us / we / me** what we can do for you.

2 Complete the dialogue with object pronouns.
A: I often come to this park. I really love _____.
B: Same here! Ranger Juan is so friendly. I like _____ a lot.
A: Yeah, and there are bears in the forest, but we never see _____.
B: Let's find someone who can help _____ see a bear.
A: Ranger Sarah gives bears medicine and food. Let's talk to _____.

5D

1 Which of 1–5 are orders (O) and which are requests (R)?
1. Please don't open the window. _____
2. Don't eat all the pizza! _____
3. Be quiet! _____
4. Open the door, please. _____
5. Listen to me! _____

2 Write the opposite instruction.
Come in. / Go away.
1. Sit down.
2. Listen to what I'm saying.
3. Please close your eyes.
4. Don't look at the board.
5. Please translate word for word.

Sounds and usual spellings

S Difficult sounds for Spanish speakers
P Difficult sounds for Portuguese speakers

▶ To listen to these words and sounds, and to practice them, go to the pronunciation section on the Richmond Learning Platform.

Vowels

/iː/ three, tree, eat, receive, believe, key, B, C, D, E, G, P, T, V, Z
/ɪ/ six, mix, it, fifty, fish, trip, lip, fix
/ʊ/ book, cook, put, could, cook, woman
/uː/ two, shoe, food, new, soup, true, suit, Q, U, W
/ɛ/ pen, ten, heavy, then, again, men, F, L, M, N, S, X
/ə/ bananas, pajamas, family, photography

/ɜr/ shirt, skirt, work, turn, learn, verb
/ɔr/ four, door, north, fourth
/ɔ/ walk, saw, water, talk, author, law
/æ/ man, fan, bad, apple
/ʌ/ sun, run, cut, umbrella, country, love
/ɑ/ hot, not, on, clock, fall, tall
/ɑr/ car, star, far, start, party, artist, R

Diphthongs

/eɪ/ plane, train, made, stay, they, A, H, J, K
/aɪ/ nine, wine, night, my, pie, buy, eyes, I, Y
/aʊ/ house, mouse, town, cloud

/ɔɪ/ toys, boys, oil, coin
/oʊ/ nose, rose, home, know, toe, road, O

☐ Voiced
☐ Unvoiced

Sounds and usual spellings

Consonants

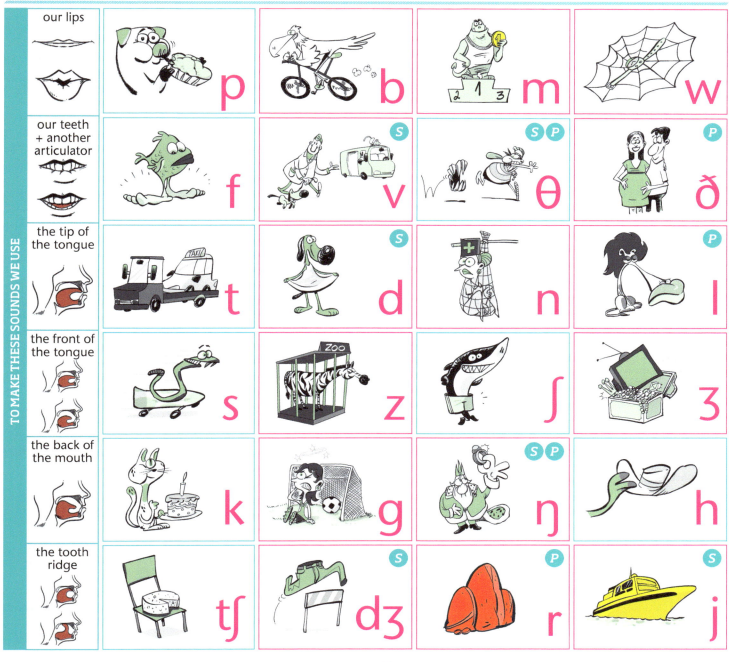

/p/	pig, pie, open, top, apple	
/b/	bike, bird, describe, able, club, rabbit	
/m/	medal, monster, name, summer	
/w/	web, watch, where, square, one	
/f/	fish, feet, off, phone, enough	
/v/	vet, van, five, have, video	
/θ/	teeth, thief, thank, nothing, mouth	
/ð/	mother, father, the, other	
/t/	truck, taxi, hot, stop, attractive	
/d/	dog, dress, made, adore, sad, middle	
/n/	net, nurse, tennis, one, sign, know	
/l/	lion, lips, long, all, old	

/s/	snake, skate, kiss, city, science
/z/	zoo, zebra, size, jazz, lose
/ʃ/	shark, shorts, action, special, session, chef
/ʒ/	television, treasure, usual
/k/	cat, cake, back, quick
/g/	goal, girl, leg, guess, exist
/ŋ/	king, ring, single, bank
/h/	hand, hat, unhappy, who
/tʃ/	chair, cheese, kitchen, future, question
/dʒ/	jeans, jump, generous, bridge
/r/	red, rock, ride, married, write
/j/	yellow, yacht, university

159

Audio script

Unit 1

▶ 1.2 Notice /ʌ/ and /uː/.
- A OK. Let's check.
- B Flag 1 is China.
- A Yes, one point for you. And country 2?
- B That's Spain.
- A Yeah! Two points.
- B Number 3 is Portugal.
- A Right again!
- B Flag 4 is the U.S.
- A Yes! That's four points now!
- B 5 is the UK.
- A Correct!
- B And 6 is Peru.
- A Right! 6 points! And number 7?
- B 7 is Canada and 8 is Argentina!
- A Yes and yes! That's 8 points for you! Very good!

▶ 1.6 Notice *This_is* connects like one word.
This_is Machu Picchu, it's_in Peru. And number 2 is the Taj Mahal. It's_in India. Number 3 is the Alhambra. It's_in Granada, Spain. Photo 4 is Maroon 5. They're from the U.S. Photo 5 is Drake and Shawn Mendes. They're Canadian. And 6 is Salma Hayek. She's Mexican. Number 7 is Serena Williams. She's American. And this_is Neymar, in picture 8. He's Brazilian.

▶ 1.7 Notice the sentence stress.
1 **Mmmm**! This **pizza** is **amazing**!
2 This is cool. **Wheeeeeeeeee**!
3 I'm so **pleased**! The **teacher** says my **work** is **excellent**.
4 I **love** New **York**. It's a **fantastic city**!
5 **Yuck**! This **coffee** is **horrible**!
6 Here's an **important story** in the **newspaper**.
7 I think **Malala** is a **very intelligent person**.
8 **China** is an **interesting country**!
9 This **restaurant** is **OK**.
10 Bill **Gates** is a **very rich person**!
11 This **group** is **ridiculous**!
12 **No**, no, no, he's a **terrible actor**! **Terrible**!

▶ 1.8 Notice /z/.
1 Oh, yeah, I agree. Neymar's an amazing soccer player.
2 The Taj Mahal – it's a really cool monument.
3 Oh, yes, Serena Williams is a rich person. Very, very rich!
4 Malala's an intelligent person, in my opinion.
5 No, I don't want to go there on vacation! It's a horrible city!
6 I think Japan is an interesting country.
7 I really like him. He's an excellent teacher.
8 I love her movies. She's a fantastic actor.

▶ 1.13 Notice the stress in these numbers is on the first syllable.
- A A hundred dollars, please.
- B OK, That's thirty, forty, fifty, sixty, seventy, eighty, ninety, a hundred. One hundred dollars.
- A Thank you, sir. Have a great day.

▶ 1.14 Notice /θ/.
1 I'm eighty-five today. Happy birthday to me!
2 My address is seventy Blue Avenue.
3 I have eleven brothers and sisters!
4 This train ticket is ninety-nine dollars!
5 Hmm, I think it's fifteen miles to Los Angeles.
6 The number after thirty-nine is forty.
7 I have sixteen classmates in my English class.
8 Thirteen hours on a plane ... I'm very tired!

▶ 1.15 Notice the **stress** in the questions.
- A Name?
- B Jack Moore.
- A **How** do you **spell** that?
- B J-A-C-K M-O-O-R-E.

2
- A Good afternoon, I'm Dieter Quinn.
- B **How** do you **spell** that?
- A D-I-E-T-E-R Q-U-I-N-N.

3
- A First and last name, please?
- B Rochelle Johns.
- A **How** do you **spell** that?
- B R-O-C-H-E-L-L-E J-O-H-N-S.

4
- A **What**'s your **name**?
- B George Wessex.
- A Can you spell that, please?
- B Sure. It's G-E-O-R-G-E W-E-S-S-E-X.

5
- A **Name**, **please**?
- B Joy Boscombe.
- A **How** do you **spell** that?
- B J-O-Y B-O-S-C-O-M-B-E.

▶ 1.16 Notice /m/ and /n/ endings and their spelling.
J = Jonathan K = Karin
- J Welcome to Minerva reservations, Canada. This is Jonathan. How can I help you today?
- K Hi, Jonathan. Can I make a reservation, please?
- J Sure, no problem. I need a little information from you, OK? Uh, what's your name?
- K Karin Spalding. That's K-A-R-I-N—Karin—S-P-A-L-D-I-N-G –Spalding.
- J Where are you from? Are you Canadian?
- K No, I'm not Canadian. I'm American, I'm from California.
- J And what's your address, Ms. Spalding?
- K 75 Kearny Drive, that's K-E-A-R-N-Y, San Francisco, CA 94133.
- J Thank you. And what's your telephone number?
- K Um, it isn't a Canadian number. It's American. OK? It's area code 415, then 675-8938.
- J Thanks. And what's your email address?
- K It's karinspalding@SPDG.com.
- J Thanks. Now, what type of room ...

▶ 1.17 Notice /k/ and /t/.
O = officer P = passenger
- O Good morning. I'm sorry, ma'am, but we need to check your backpack, please.
- P No problem. Here you are.
- O OK, let's see. A wallet, a laptop, keys, hmm ... a phone, a pencil, an umbrella, hmm ... what's this?
- P Oh, this is a lipstick. Look!
- O I see ... Are these glasses yours?
- P Yes, they are.
- O Right, and what are those?
- P These are my earrings.
- O OK ... And what's that?
- P Come on! That's a sandwich!
- O Exactly! You can't enter this country with food, ma'am!!
- P Uh-uh. Sorry, it's my first time here.
- O I need to take that. Thank you

▶ 1.19 Notice /i/ and /iː/.
R = Rosa J = Jake E = Ed L = Lara
1
- R Is this your sandwich, Jake?
- J Hmmm ...Yes, it is. It's good!
- R And are these your keys?
- J Yes, they are, thanks.

2
- E Is that your laptop, Rosa?
- R No, it isn't. Is it your laptop, Lara?
- L Yes, it is! That's my laptop!! It's new!

3
- R & J Hey! Those are our potato chips!
- L Come on, Ed! These are their chips! Stop eating them!
- E Sorry.

4
- E Where are my glasses?
- R Er ... Are these your glasses, Ed?
- E Yes, they are. Thanks. How do they look?

5
- J Are these your earrings, Rosa?
- R No, they aren't my earrings. They're awful! Are they your earrings, Lara?
- L Yes, they are. Hmpf! Thanks.

6
- L That's someone's phone!
- E I think it's her phone. Hey, Rosa! Is that your phone?
- R No, it's isn't. My phone's new.
- L I think it's his phone.
- E Oh, yes, that's my phone ... Er ... Hi mom!

▶ 1.21 Notice /b/, /g/ and /z/.
1 They're big and shiny ... The earrings.
2 They're big and blue. There are two in the picture ... The sofas.
3 They're small and gray ... The glasses.
4 It's not big or small, it's new, and it's on the table ... The laptop.
5 It's small and black, and it's on the sofa ...The phone.

▶ 1.23 Notice /dʒ/ and the sentence stress.
M = Mark J = Justine
- M Good evening! **Welcome** to **Conference Registration**. **My** name's **Mark**. **How** can I **help** you **today**?
- J I need to register for the conference – your website isn't working.
- M Certainly. I just need some information about you. First, **What's** your **name**?
- J Justine Wallace.
- M **How** do you **spell** that?
- J J-U-S-T-I-N-E W-A-L-L-A-C-E.
- M And **what's** your **address**, Ms. Wallace?
- J **18 Jeff**rey Drive, that's J-E-F-F-R-E-Y Drive, Denver, Colorado. **Zip** code **80202**.
- M **Thank** you, and **what's** your **phone** number?
- J **720** is the **area** code and the number is **988-3405**.
- M **Thanks**. And what's your **email** address?
- J It's **jwallace26** at **webmail** dot **com**.
- M **Thanks**, now, and can I **ask** about your **nationality**? **Where** are you from?
- J I'm **American**.
- M OK – so, you're all set – you're **registered** for the **conference**.

160

Audio script

1.24 Notice /h/.
A Hi Judy! How are you?
B Good, thanks. What about you? What's new?
A Not much. Things are good.
B So are you ready for the meeting? I hear …

1.26 Notice the sentence stress.
1
A Here's your gift! Happy Birthday!
B Thank you!
A You're welcome.
2
A Excuse me.
B Oh, I'm sorry.
3
A Oops, I'm sorry.
B Don't worry about it.
4
A See you later!
B Bye for now!
5
A We have a great fish special today.
B Excuse me. Can you say that again, please?
A Sure … I said we have a great fish special today.
6
A D'ya wanna order now?
B I don't understand.
C Oh, sorry. Are you ready to order?

Unit 2

2.1 Notice to /tə/ and to a /tu:wə/.
I = interviewer
I When do you go to these places?
A I go to a café every day before class for a coffee.
B I go to church on Sundays.
C I go to the gym after school.
D I usually go home after work.
E I go to a party on Saturdays.
F I go to school Monday through Friday, and Saturday morning, too!
G I go to the grocery store on Saturdays.
H I go to work at eight o'clock.

2.2 Notice stress on days of the week.
1 Sunday, lovely Sunday!
2 Oh, no! Tomorrow's Monday. School! Yuk!
3 Gee, it's only Tuesday – four more days of work.
4 I have an important meeting on Wednesday.
5 Only two more days of work – it's Thursday.
6 Today is Friday. Let's go to a bar after work!
7 Great! It's Saturday! My favorite day! No more work for the weekend!

2.4 Notice /ɜr/.
I = interviewer W = woman M = man
I Hi, I'm doing a survey about sleeping habits. What time do you get up?
W Uh, um, at six in the morning. I go to school at six forty-five.
I Thanks. And what time do you go to bed?
W Hmm. At around ten p.m., during the week. Maybe at twelve midnight on Friday and Saturday.
I So you get about eight hours sleep a night?
W Yeah, that's it … Bye!
I Thanks.
I Hello, we're doing a survey about working hours. What time do you go to work?
M Hmm … I go to work at eight thirty a.m.

I Every day?
M No, no. From Monday to Friday. I don't work on Saturdays and Sundays.
I And when do you get home from work?
M Well, I usually get home at around six fifteen p.m. OK? Bye!

2.6 Notice /eɪ/ and word stress.
Well, I wake up at around six thirty a.m., but I don't get up immediately. I stay in bed for three or four minutes, then I get up and make my bed. Then I exercise for thirty minutes. After that, I take a shower, shave, get dressed and have breakfast – coffee, juice and cereal.
Then I brush my teeth and, finally, leave home at around eight a.m.

2.7 Notice /s/ and /z/.
He wakes up at eight a.m., but he doesn't get up. He sleeps again and then he gets up at 8:50 a.m., but he doesn't wake up. After he wakes up he makes his bed. Then he exercises and he shaves. After that, he doesn't take a shower, he doesn't brush his teeth, and he doesn't get dressed!

2.9 Notice the intonation at the end of each question.
1
A What's your full name?
B I'm Miguel Hernandez. But please call me Mickey.
2
A OK. And … are you Spanish?
B Yes, I am. I'm from Valencia.
3
A Where do you live?
B In Madrid, I work there. It's an amazing city!
4
A Do you live with your parents?
B No, I don't. I live with my girlfriend, Monica.
5
A Where exactly in the U.S. do you plan to travel to?
B Alaska. They say it's a beautiful place.
6
A Do you know anyone in Alaska?
B Yes, my sister lives there.

2.10 Notice the intonation at the end of each question.
M = Miguel W = woman
W Hm … Who's this?
M That's my brother, Juan.
W Uh-huh. Does he play soccer?
M Yes, he does! He loves soccer.
W And who's that?
M That's my sister, Martina.
W So you have a sister! Where does she live?
M In Alaska. And, those are my parents.
W Wow, Alaska! And, do your parents live there too?
M No, they live in Barcelona.

Review 1

R1.2 Notice /ə/ in the articles and prepositions.
My name's Carla, I'm 17, and I live in La Floresta, a small town in Spain about 13 km from Barcelona. I live with my mom and dad and my six brothers and sisters, so, with me, that's a total of nine people in our house. It's a big family – I have over 40 cousins!
I'm a student and I study at the University of Barcelona. I get up at 6 a.m. every day. It takes me 50 minutes to get to school, which starts at 8 a.m. In my free time, I like watching movies, and my favorite actors are Penelope Cruz and Jennifer Lawrence. I usually go to the movies on Monday night after school.

Unit 3

3.1 Notice /j/ and /dʒ/.
I = interviewer M = meteorologist
I You're a meteorologist, please tell us about the symbols that are used to represent weather.
M Well, when we use weather symbols we try to use symbols that everyone will understand. This yellow circle means the sun, or sunny weather. A cloud means cloudy, obviously, and this symbol means a wind or windy. The gray cloud is for fog or foggy weather. The cloud with these little lines means rain or rainy weather. And the white cloud with stars means snow or snowy conditions.
I So, it's easy to see what the weather is like just from the symbol?
M That's right.
I What about temperature?
M We usually use the words hot, warm, cool, or cold.

3.2 Notice /w/ and /v/.
A OK, in this photo, the weather is warm.
B Yes, it's hot and sunny.
A Maybe it's Cancún?
B And in this picture it's very, very hot!
A Yes, and it isn't raining. It's very dry.

3.3 Notice /d/ and /t/.
B = Bob M = Mary J = Joe
B Everywhere, the weather is … weird! Take the Amazon rainforest, for example. It's usually very rainy there, but now … no rain for three months! The Amazon river is down by 10 meters. It's weird! From the forest to the desert: the Atacama Desert is usually hot and sunny 350 days a year. This year, the days and nights are cool and cloudy. It's weird! And how's the weather in Chicago, the Windy City? Mary, tell us. What's the weather like in Chicago?
M Well, Bob, no wind for us! This month, every morning, it's cool and foggy. It's weird!
B Thanks Mary. Let's go to the Alps. Those beautiful mountains. What's the weather usually like there? It's snowy, right? And what's it like this year? Tell us Joe?
J Uh-huh. It's warm and there's absolutely no snow. Skiing is impossible. It's weird!
B How about Cancún, and the fantastic beaches? Well, tourists go to Cancún to enjoy the hot weather but this summer: it's cold. Really cold. It's weird! What's the weather like where you are? Any weird weather stories? Contact us to tell us …

3.4 Notice s = /s/ or /z/.
M = Maddie E = Eli S = Susan R = Rita
C = caller Mi = Michael
E Hello?
M Eli? This is Maddie. Are you busy?
E Actually, yes. I'm cooking dinner. What's up?
M Oh, no problem. Call you later.
E OK, bye.

161

S Susan.
M Hi, Susan. This is Maddie.
S Oh, hi, Maddie. Sorry, I'm running in the park. I can't hear you. Can I call you later?
M Sure, Susan. Talk to you later.
S Bye.
M OK, uh, bye. Not my day today, is it? Let me try Rita.
R Rita Rogers speaking.
M Hey, Rita!
R Maddie, darling. How are you doing?
M Great.
R Excuse me. Can you tell me where the butter is, please? Sorry, Maddie, I'm buying groceries. What's up?
M Well, I have …
R Oh, and the milk? Uh, sorry, Maddie.
M Oh, you're busy now. Don't worry. Bye.
R Bye, darling. Nice talking to you.
M So, Rita is busy, too. Maybe Michael? Let me try him. Uh … the line's busy …
M Ooh, someone's calling. Maybe one of my friends is finally free now. Hello?
C Gregory Hanes, please?
M Uh, I'm sorry, you have the wrong number.
C Oh, sorry. I'll dial again.
M Humph. Typical! Well, let me call Michael again.
Mi Hi, Maddie.
M Hi, Michael. Are you running?
Mi No, I'm not running! I'm riding a bike and my battery's dying. Call you later?
M Of course … Bye.

3.5 Notice the connections for similar sounds.
M = Maddie S = Sean
M I don't believe_this. One more call. That's it.
S Hey, Maddie. Long time_no see. How are things?
M Good! Uh, Sean, are you busy?
S Um, well, I'm doing_my homework.
M Oh, never min …
S … but I'm just finishing. What are your plans?
M I have two tickets to today's game. L.A. Lakers and Houston Rockets. It starts at three o'clock.
S So we have thirty minutes! Let's go!
M Are you saying yes?
S Of course! Why are you surprised?
M You have no idea … Meet you at the subway station. Let's go!

3.9 Notice /n/ and /ŋ/.
J = Jennifer M = Marisa
J Hey, Marisa! Hi! It's great to see you.
M You too, Jennifer.
J What are you doing these days?
M I'm studying.
J Oh? Are you studying art? You're such a good painter.
M No, I'm studying biology.
J Really? And … er … where are you living?
M I'm living with my parents.
J Are you still dating Kevin?
M No, I'm not dating Kevin anymore. He's living in New York now. I'm dating a guy called Steve.
J Oh, that's nice. [awkward silence] Well … it was great to see you.
M You too. Bye.
J Bye, Marisa.

3.10 Notice /eɪ/ and /aɪ/.
S = Sammy M = Marsha L = Lucinda
K = KoolKat D = Dadofthree
B = BBBaxter
S What do you think of technology?
M It's dangerous. Social media companies are changing the way we see privacy. Everyone is getting access to our personal information.
L I don't like a lot of the new video games. They're getting more violent and it makes people act more violently.
K People are going out less and spending more time alone with technology. We don't know our neighbors.
D People today are becoming obsessed with things! They want new clothes, new cars, new electronic devices, and they can buy it all online.
B My kids are spending more and more time on their devices and online, especially on social media. I don't know what to do. They panic when they don't have their phone with them. They just want to look at their phones.

3.12 Notice have to /f/ and kind of /v/.
M = Mark L = Linda
M Hey Linda, what are you doing? It's one a.m.!
L Oh it's you, Mark. Umm … I'm working on this report. I have to turn it in tomorrow.
M Ah. Is it a big report?
L Yep, I still need to do three more pages.
M Ooosh. You tired?
L Yeah. Kind of.

Unit 4

4.2 Notice /i/ and /ɪ/.
T = Tasha M = Mac
T Today's exciting events at the Olympic Games include basketball, soccer, tennis, volleyball, cycling, running, and swimming … Wow! Tell us about it, Mac!
M Hi Tasha! Yeah, it's July 2nd, and … well, what a day of sports at the Olympics! A very exciting morning here at the Olympic complex. First we have basketball at the Olympic Arena. It's the semi-final between Cuba and Russia, at 9:00 a.m. Then, at 9:30, we have tennis, men's doubles, at the Central Courts. At 10:00 a.m. at the Olympic Stadium we have soccer, Uruguay versus Italy. What an interesting game! After that, at 10:30, it's time for cycling at the Igloo. The men's 5,000 meters final! And at 11:00 at North Park we have women's volleyball, the U.S. and Australia going for a bronze medal. And that's just this morning! Tasha, it's hard to decide what to watch!

4.4 Notice intonation = speaker's emotion.
I = interviewer W = woman
I Excuse me, miss? Can I ask you a question?
W Yes?
I What's your favorite sport?
W Skiing. I love↗ to ski.
I Nice↗! Thanks.
W You're welcome.

I = interviewer B = boy
I Hi, uh, do you have a moment?
B Uh, OK.
I What's your favorite sport?
B It's golf↘. Absolutely, golf↗. To play and↘ to watch. Best↗ game in the world↘!

W Thanks.

I = interviewer W = woman
W Uh, sorry. Excuse me!
I Sorry, er, hello! Do you have time to answer one question?
W Uh, what question?
I It's for a survey. What's your favorite sport?
W Let me think. It's definitely not↘ soccer. I hate↘ soccer.
I OK, but what sport do you like?
W Er … is skateboarding a sport?
I Well, yes, I guess so.
W So it's skateboarding↗. I love↗ it.
I OK, thanks then!
W Is that all?
I Yes. Thanks very much!
W Oh, no problem!

I = interviewer M = man
I Excuse me?
M Uh? What?
I Sorry, but, er … Do you have time to answer one question?
M Uh, I guess↗. But only one↘!
I What's your favorite sport?
M To watch or to play?
I To watch and to play.
M Well, I like to watch baseball↘ on TV↘, but, you know, I don't play↗ baseball. I love to surf↘. I go surfing↗ every weekend.
I Watch baseball, and surf. Thanks a lot.
M You're welcome. Bye↗.

4.5 Notice the intonation in yes / no ❓ and Wh- ❓.
J = Janet M = Mark
J Hi, Mark. My name is Janet and I'm your instructor.
M Oh hi Janet. How's it going?↘
J Good. I need to ask you a few questions. Is that OK?↗
M Sure.
J What's your full name?↘
M Mark Swift. S-W-I-F-T.
J Swift, OK. How old are you, Mark?↘
M I'm 23.
J OK. Can you run two kilometers?↗
M Run? No, I can't. I don't think I can walk two kilometers! That's why I'm here.
J OK, great! How about swimming?↘ Can you swim?↗
M Er, yes, I can, but not very well. I need lessons.
J We can help you with that. Let's see … Can you ride a bike?↗
M A bike? Yes, I can. But I don't like it.
J Hmm. OK. Can you play tennis?↗
M No, no, I can't play tennis at all. I hate tennis.
J I see. Well, so you can run in the gym every day, and our swimming lessons are…

4.6 Notice /aʊ/ and the connections.
Let_us pick_up our books_and our pens. They_are_our most powerful weapons. One child, one teacher, one book, and one pen can change the world. Education_is the_only solution. Education first. Thank_you.

Audio script

4.8 Notice pronunciation of can in ❓ and can/can't in ➕ ➖.

I = interviewer M = man W = woman

1
I Can you dance?
M I can't dance very well, but my wife can. She's a very good dancer.

2
I Who can cook well in your family?
W Not me! But, my father can cook really well. His food is delicious.

3
I What about your friends? What sports can your best friend play?
M Hmmm, my best friend can't play baseball or volleyball. He doesn't like team sports.

4
I And winter sports? Can you skate?
W I can skate, but I can't ski at all. Skiing is too difficult!

5
I Can your friends play soccer?
M For sure! My friends can play soccer really well. They play every weekend.

6
I Can you do any martial arts?
W Yes, I can.
I What can you do?
W Tae Kwondo.

4.10 Notice /æ/ and /ɛ/.

J = Joel A = applicant

J Hello. I'm Joel Clinton. I have your curriculum vitae here and I want to ask you some questions.
A Sure.
J There is no information about your language abilities. How many languages can you speak?
A Er, apart from English, one. I speak a little Spanish.
J ¿Como estás?
A What?
J Yes, I can see you speak very little Spanish. Anyway, I'm also interested in your athletic abilities. Can you play any sports?
A Uh, a little, yes.
J What sports can you play?
A I can play volleyball and tennis, but not very well.
J Not perfect, but OK. One more question: can you text fast?
A Yes, I think so.
J How many words a minute can you text?
A I don't know – about 40, I think. But wait? Why are these questions relevant? Isn't this a job interview for a position as a babysitter?
J No, I want a nanny, and I want my son to have the best education!
A And how old is your son?
J Two!

4.16 Notice the /t/ and silent t.

S = sales clerk J = Jason

S The fitting rooms are over there.
J Thank you.
S Do you need any help, sir?
J No, no, it's perfect. What do you think? Blue is Jackson's favorite color. Isn't it, Jackson? Back in you go!
S And for you, sir? We have wonderful T-shirts, pants, jackets, suits …

Review 2

R2.2 Notice /r/ at beginning of words and /r/ at end of words.

G = Gale R = Ricky

G And here with us today we have the Paralympic swimmer, Ricky Pietersen. Hello, Ricky.
R Hi, Gale. It's nice to be here.
G So, Ricky, what's your favorite sport?
R Well, I love swimming, of course!
G How about other sports? Do you like soccer?
R Yes, I love to watch my team play.
G Cool! What else do you like doing when you're not swimming or watching your team?
R Well, I like to help young kids with disabilities.
G That's great. And a final question: what is your next big challenge?
R I'm working hard to prepare for the next Paralympic Games. I want to beat my own record.
G Well, thank you for talking to us today, Ricky.
R Thank you, Gale!

Unit 5

5.1 Notice /ə/ and /ʌ/.

A = adviser V = visitor

A Places to go out near here? Well, there's a bar, and a club, and a hotel. And there's a nice museum, and a park. And there's a very good restaurant. And a small stadium, oh, and an old theater.
V Great, thank you – that sounds good.

5.3 Notice the word stress.

Welcome to Louisville, the largest city in Kentucky! It's a great place to visit. Situated on the Ohio river with a population of about 750,000, it's the City of Parks. There are 122 parks in the city!
Downtown there are seven museums, and three theaters, plus the Louisville Ballet, Orchestra and Opera.
Louisville is home to the famous Kentucky Derby horse race, sometimes called the Greatest Two Minutes in Sports! There's a famous racetrack and a museum at Churchill Downs. There's also a football stadium and a baseball stadium in the city. If you like shopping, there are three enormous shopping malls to choose from. And for readers, there's a fantastic public library with branches all over town.
Kentucky is the home of KFC (Kentucky Fried Chicken), but we don't only eat fried chicken! There are restaurants of all kinds here.
There aren't any public swimming pools in downtown Louisville, but there are six pools in the city, so everything is easy. And of course there are bars, clubs, and four multi-screen movie theaters. And seven world-class hotels, just in the downtown area. The only thing you won't find here? There are no unfriendly people – just friends you don't know yet!
So, come to Louisville – for relaxation and fun!

5.6 Notice /ɪ/ and /aɪ/. Notice the position of also and too.

Well, I love playing video games. It's my favorite thing in the world. I also love going out with my friends. I like to shop and I like to eat out. And, um, I like blogging too. And I don't mind going to work. I also don't mind cooking – it's fun with a friend, but I don't like going to the gym very much. I don't like watching TV either, but the one thing I really hate is cleaning. I hate cleaning the house! What about you? Are you similar?

5.9 Notice main sentence stress on content words and at the end of phrases.

N = Natalie P = presenter

N I'm Natalie and I'm ten years old and I love to sing. I've been singing ever since I was four. I sing at school, I sing at home, I sometimes sing when I'm eating my dinner! I would like to be a singer and a diva and I definitely want to be like Beyoncé.
P Hello darling.
N Hello.
P What's your name and how old are you?
N My name is Natalie and I'm ten years old.
P And what are you doing today?
N Well, I'm going to sing a song called 'No One' from Alicia Keys.
P OK, yeah – I know that one. Good luck, darling.

5.12 Notice the pronunciation of the -ing /ŋ/ form.

J = Josh E = Emily

J Let's go on vacation together, Emily. What do you like doing on vacation?
E Well, I love sunbathing and swimming. How about you?
J Hmmm, well, I don't really like swimming or sunbathing, but I love snorkeling and kayaking. I sometimes like to take a class or to visit the museums to discover more about where I am.
E Do you? I prefer reading novels and eating out and dancing, nothing cultural for me.
J What about sightseeing?
E I like sightseeing, but not too much.
J And camping? Do you like camping?
E Not really. I hate shopping, especially buying souvenirs, and cooking and hiking when I'm on vacation. I just want to relax.
J Those are the things I love doing on vacation! Hmm …

5.17 Notice the pronunciation of object pronouns in speech.

Hi Lori! Thanks for house sitting for us during our vacation. Hope you don't have any problems.
Just a few things to remember. Er, when you come in, please pick up the mail↘ and put it on the table↘.
Um, yeah, please open the windows↘ and close them again every day↘ – oh, and water the plants every day↘. Also, don't forget the lights and air conditioning↘ – turn them off when you go out↘.
Feed Salt and Pepper (that's the cats!) and Chips (that's the dog!) in the morning and evening↘, but please don't give them too much food↘. Oh and, don't forget to give them some water.↘
Please, walk Chips in the morning and afternoon↘. But please don't take him near the road↘. He's nervous of cars. And please, please, don't let the cats out.↘
Call me if you have any questions↘ and please tell us if the cats or Chips escape↘. Thanks again! See you in two weeks. Have fun!↘ Bye.

163

5.22 Notice st- at the beginning of a word.

1

M = man W = woman

M Excuse me.
W H!. How're you doing?
M Oh, hi. Good, thanks, er, where's the mall?
W It's in front of you on Market Street. Cross here at the stoplight.
M Thanks.
W No problem. Have a nice day!

2

W = woman M = man

W Excuse me. Is there a movie theater around here?
M Yes, there is. Go straight on Market Street and turn right on Fourth Street. Go straight for one block and the movie theater's on the corner of Fourth and Mission Street.

3

M = man W = woman

M Excuse me. Do you know where the library is?
W Excuse me?
M The library?
W Ah, yes. Um, er, I know! Go straight on Market Street for four blocks. Turn right on Grove Street at the stop sign. Then, um, er, go straight for one block and the library is on the right.
M Thank you.

4

M1, M2, M3 = man 1, man 2, man 3

M1 Um, er, excuse me, are there any ...
M2 Sorry, my friend. No time, bye!
M1 Hmpf. Excuse me. Are there any bookstores near here?
M3 Yes, there are.
M1 Good, er, where are they?
M3 Oh yes, sorry. There's one on Market Street. Go straight for about four blocks. The bookstore's on your left. Before the stop sign.
M1 Sorry, can you say that again?
M3 I'm sorry. There's one on Market Street. Go straight for about four blocks. The bookstore's on your left. Before the stop sign. OK?
M1 Er, thank you.

PAUL SELIGSON
TOM ABRAHAM
CRIS GONTOW

2nd edition

English ID

Workbook 1

1

1.1 Are you Canadian?

1 Put these words in the correct column.

Africa   America   Asia   Australia   Brazil   Canada   Chile   Europe   India   Korea

Countries	Continents

2 ▶ 1.1 Add **n**, **an**, or **ian** to make the adjective. Listen, check, and repeat the countries and adjectives with the correct stress.

3 Read a–e and write the country or nationality.
a I'm from Milan, in the north of ___Italy___.
b I come from a large country in Asia. The capital of my country is Delhi. I'm _____.
c My native language is Mandarin. I'm _____.
d My new phone is a Samsung. It's from _____.
e The famous Machu Picchu ruins are in my country. I'm _____.

4 ▶ 1.2 Listen and complete dialogues 1–5.

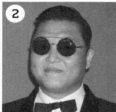

1 A ___Is___ Rachel Griffiths Amer___ican___?
  B No, she ___isn't___. She _____ Austr_____.
2 A _____ you Chinese?
  B No, I _____. I'm Kor_____.
3 A _____ Kunal Nayyar Per_____?
  B No, he's Ind_____. He _____ from Delhi.
4 A Are they Ameri_____?
  B No, _____. They _____ Bri_____.
5 A Is Javier Bardem Mex_____?
  B No, he _____. He _____ Spa_____.

5 Check ✓ the correct sentences. Correct the mistakes in the wrong ones.
a Maradona is a̶ interesting person. *an*
b Shanghai is a fantastic city. ✓
c My brother is an horrible singer.
d You are a excellent actor.
e She is an OK writer.
f It is a special city.

6 Order the words in a–e to make sentences.
a terrible / I / a / *Star Wars* / is / think / movie / .
_____
b is / player / Luis Suárez / excellent / an / .
_____
c I / is / São Paulo / a / city /great / think / .
_____
d country / think / India / interesting / I / is / an / .
_____
e actor / Chris Pratt / cool / a / is / .
_____

7 **Make it personal** Write three ⊕ and three ⊖ opinions. Use these words to help you.

an actor   a soccer player   a movie
a musician   a restaurant   a song   your city

⊕ *Star Wars is a great movie.*
⊖ *My city isn't an excellent place.*

Connect

Use one of your opinions in **7** to write a short tweet.

1.2 How do you spell your last name?

1 ▶1.3 **Listen and write eight famous TV channels.**
   a ___
   b ___
   c ___
   d ___
   e ___
   f ___
   g ___
   h ___

2 **Cross out the word with the different vowel sound in a–g.**
   a a plane – a train – are
   b a shoe – go – two
   c a car – a star – a name
   d ten – a tree – three
   e a pen – eight – twelve
   f nine – wine – six
   g one – go – a rose

3 ▶1.4 **Match these pairs to the correct vowel sound group a–g in 2. Listen to check.**
   - [d] she – me
   - [ ] hi – five
   - [ ] a guitar – a party
   - [ ] no – a nose
   - [ ] blue – you
   - [ ] a name – Spain
   - [ ] ten – yes

4 **Complete the puzzle with vowels to reveal the numbers 1–10.**

5 ▶1.5 **Listen and complete dialogues 1–4. Calculate the final number.**

   1 A Excuse me. Can I help you?
      B Hi, these shorts and these sandals, please.
      A OK. The shorts are _____ euros and the sandals _____ euros. The total is _____ euros.
   2 A Next please.
      B A train ticket to New York, please.
      A New York. That's _____ dollars.
      B Wow! Er ... OK. Here's _____.
      A Thanks. Here's your ticket and _____ dollars.
   3 A How much are the donuts?
      B _____ cents each.
      A OK! Can I have _____, please?
      B That's _____ dollars. There you go. Enjoy!
   4 A Valentine's Day is going to be perfect, huh?!
      B Yep! _____ red roses and a meal in a restaurant. And the roses cost _____ dollars each.
      A That's _____ dollars! That's ridiculous!

6 ▶1.6 **Listen to check the final number.**

7 **Make it personal** **Complete the conversation with your details.**
   A Hi! My name's Marty Anders, nice to meet you. I'm American and I'm from New York. I'm 14.
   B Hi! Nice _____ you. My first name's _____ and my last name's _____. I'm _____. I'm from _____. I'm _____.

1.3 What's your email address?

1 ▶ 1.7 Listen and complete the form.

| First name: |
| Last name: |
| Hotel address: Hotel   ,   Sea Parade. |
| Phone: |
| Email: @   .com |

2 ▶ 1.8 Ask questions using **what**. Follow the model.

Model: *Name.*
You: *What's your name?*
Model: *Full name.*
You: *What's your full name?*

3 Write questions.
a _____ Robert Smith
b _____ New York City
c _____ 457-3903
d _____ 4 North Avenue
e _____ smithrob@gmail.com

4 **Make it personal** Answer questions a–e in **3** and complete a form about yourself.

5 Order the letters to spell five common objects. Then find the secret object.

6 Put these words in the correct plural box.

address   backpack   city   country   earring
glass   key   nationality   phone   sandwich

| + S |
| + ES |
| –Y + IES |

7 ▶ 1.9 Circle the correct word in dialogues 1–5.

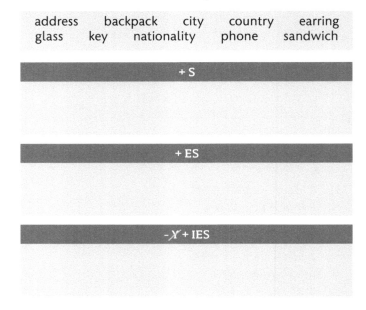

1 A **This** / **That** is my new boyfriend.
   B Oh, wow! He's cool.
2 A **This** / **That** is my family's apartment. The view is fantastic.
   B Wow! You are lucky. I can't see anything from my apartment.
3 A **This** / **These** are my new earrings. Do you like **it** / **them**?
   B Ummm. **They** / **It** are … interesting.
4 A Excuse me. What are **these** / **those**?
   B **It** / **They** are mangos. Very fresh, very delicious. Two for a dollar.
5 A **This** / **These** roses are for you. I love you!
   B Oh, Fabio! **They** / **These** are beautiful! Thank you.

1.4 Are these your glasses?

1 Complete the photo comments with *their*, *our*, *your*, *his*, or *her*.

1. This is a photo of Tim and me on _____ vacation.
2. This is Mark with _____ horrible new sunglasses.
3. Sorry, are these _____ sunglasses?
4. Lions with _____ babies … Fantastic!

2 Correct the mistakes in a–f.
  a This is Peter and her girlfriend, Sharon.
  b You are pretty. What's her name?
  c Anna loves his pretty new earrings.
  d These are ours chairs.
  e What are they're names?
  f Are these yours keys?

3 Match phrases a–k to the answers.

a	The American president lives there.
b	The Argentinian president lives there.
c	A famous Colombian singer.
d	World famous blue jeans.
e	A fictional black and white cartoon dog.
f	Mix red and blue to make this color.
g	The colors of the Spanish flag.
h	A little orange clown fish.
i	A red, green, or yellow fruit.
j	He lives with the dog in **e**.
k	A Black Eyed Peas song.

Shakira
Charlie Brown
The White House
Purple
Red and yellow
An apple
Levi's
"Where is the love?"
Snoopy
The Pink House
Nemo

4 ▶1.10 Describe the objects. Follow the model.
Model: *Car. Blue.*
You: *It's a blue car.*

Model: *Song. Famous.*
You: *It's a famous song.*

Connect
Write short descriptions of the last three photos you took on your phone.

1.5 What's your full name?

1 Read the forms and answer a–f.

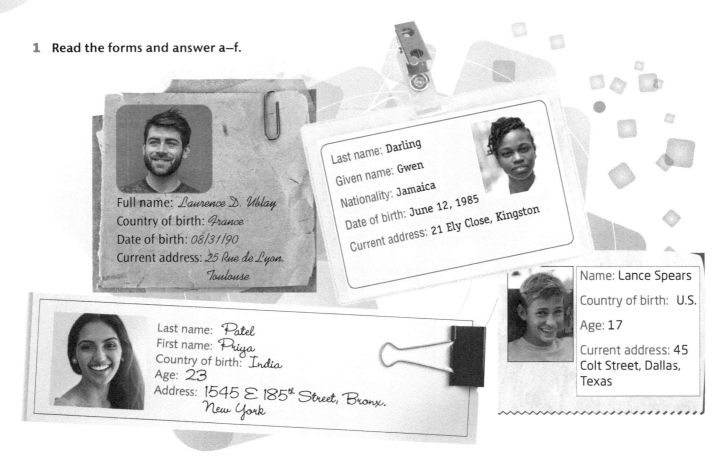

a What nationality is Lance?

b Where's Gwen from?

c What's Laurence's date of birth?

d What's the Indian woman's last name?

e How old is Priya?

f What's Lance's address?

2 ▶1.11 **Make it personal** Listen and answer the questions.

 Connect
*Use your phone to record your answers.
Send them to a classmate or your teacher.*

3 ▶1.12 **Listen and choose the best response.**
   a Fine, thanks. / Not really.
   b Not so good. / Not much.
   c Bye, for now. / Hi!
   d I'm well. / You're welcome.
   e I'm sorry. / Nothing much.
   f Oh, sorry. / Sure.

4 ▶1.12 **Cover 3. Listen again and answer. Follow the model.**
   Model: *How are you?*
   You: *Fine, thanks.*

Can you remember ...
- 8 countries and nationalities? SB→p. 6
- 12 adjectives to give your opinion? SB→p. 7
- the 26 letters of the alphabet? SB→p. 8
- numbers 1–100? SB→p. 9
- 5 *Wh-* questions? SB→p. 10
- 11 everyday objects? SB→p. 11
- 10 colors and 6 adjectives? SB→p. 13
- 6 greetings? SB→p. 15

2.1 When do you get up?

1 **Complete a–g with *to a*, *to the*, *to*, or *–*. For a–e, check the true sentences. Answer f and g.**
   a I go _____ small café in the mornings.
   b We go _____ grocery store on weekends.
   c I go _____ gym every day.
   d I want to go _____ party tonight, but I have to go _____ work!
   e I go _____ home after school.
   f Do you go _____ school on Saturdays?
   g Do you go _____ church?

2 **▶ 2.1 Copy the rhythm. Follow the model.**
   Model: *home after school.*
   You: *I go home after school.*
   Model: *work on Monday.*
   You: *I go to work on Monday.*

3 **Read the article and match the ancient gods to the days.**

ORIGINS OF A NAME

The names for the days of the week in some modern languages come from the gods of Ancient Rome. For example, *Day of Venus*, the Roman goddess of love, is the modern Spanish *Viernes*. With the expansion of the Roman Empire, the Germanic and Nordic people adopted the Roman practice. They modified the system to use the corresponding gods from their culture, like *Frige*, the Nordic goddess of love. So both *Friday* and *Viernes* are the *Day of Love*!

a	The Sun	Monday
b	Mercury and *Woden*: music and poetry	Tuesday
c	Venus and *Frige*: love	Wednesday
d	The Moon	Thursday
e	Mars and *Tiw*: combat	Friday
f	Jupiter and *Thor*: Chief of Gods	Saturday
g	Saturn: Time	Sunday

4 **Reread. Answer questions a–c.**
   a How many days have names from Nordic gods?
      ☐ 3   ☐ 4   ☐ 5
   b Which planet gives its name to a day in English?
      ☐ Venus   ☐ Mercury   ☐ Saturn
   c What is the most romantic day of the week?
      ☐ Wednesday   ☐ Thursday   ☐ Friday

5 **▶ 2.2 Listen and check the times you hear, a–e.**

   a ☐ 6:15   ☐ 6:45   *It's six forty-five.*
   b ☐ 6:30   ☐ 7:30   _____
   c ☐ 5:00   ☐ 4:00   _____
   d ☐ 12:15   ☐ 12:45   _____
   e ☐ 2:45   ☐ 3:15   _____

6 **Write the times you don't hear in 5.**

7 **Order the words in a–f to make questions.**
   a ? / you / do / time / go / school / to / what
      _____
   b ? / time / go / you / to / what / bed / do
      _____
   c ? / what / work / time / go / you / to / do
      _____
   d ? / do / home / time / what / you / get
      _____
   e ? / do / you / up / what / get / time
      _____
   f ? / to / what / you / gym / the / do / go / time
      _____

8 **🎤 Make it personal** Answer questions a–f in 7.
   I go to school at 7.

📶 Connect

*Use your phone to record your answers.
Send them to a classmate or your teacher.*

2.2 What do you do in the mornings?

1 Match a–h to the second column to make phrases from the Student's Book.

a brush — a shower
b get — the bed
c get — breakfast
d have — dressed
e leave — my teeth
f make — home
g take — up
h wake — up

2 **Make it personal** Put the phrases in **1** in order for your morning routine.

3 ▶2.3 Read the blog post and listen. Fill in the gaps with the phrases.

| immediately | at around | for twenty minutes | at six thirty | for around |

My Morning!

I'm Alan. I'm an Olympic athlete and this is my morning routine! My alarm clock wakes me up _____ and I get out of bed _____. I exercise _____ thirty minutes **and then** I take a shower _____ and my mom prepares my breakfast. I get dressed and **after that** I have breakfast, brush my teeth, and leave the house _____ eight o'clock. **Then** I go to the gym for more exercise! I don't have time to make my bed, my mom does that for me, too. I love my mom!

4 Reread. True (T) or False (F)?
a Alan stays in bed after he wakes up.
b Alan exercises for half an hour.
c Alan takes a shower before he eats.
d Alan brushes his teeth after breakfast.
e Alan makes his bed in the morning.
f Alan leaves the house and goes to the gym.

5 **Make it personal** Write a paragraph about your morning routine using the **bold** linkers in the blog post in **3**.

6 Complete song lines A–H with *love*, *loves*, *don't love*, or *doesn't love*.

A "I _____ you like a love song, baby."
 Selena Gomez and The Scene

B "She _____ you yeah, yeah, yeah." *The Beatles*

C "When a man _____ a woman, he can do no wrong." *Percy Sledge*

D "I _____ (–) you like I loved you yesterday."
 My Chemical Romance

E "I don't ever wanna to feel like I did that day. Take me to the place I _____, take me all the way." *Red Hot Chili Peppers*

F "I _____ to _____, but my baby just _____ to dance." *Tina Charles*

G "I _____ rock 'n' roll." *Joan Jett and The Blackhearts*

H "As the nights go by, makes you want to die. Because your baby _____ (–) you anymore." *The Carpenters*

7 ▶2.4 Say the opposite. Follow the model.

Model: *I love you.*
You: *I don't love you.*

Model: *He doesn't have breakfast.*
You: *He has breakfast.*

2.3 Who do you live with?

1 ▶2.5 **Listen and complete the family tree with these names.**

   Alexandra   Ann   Camilla   Edward
   Peter   Richard   Sandra

2 **Look at the family tree. True (T) or False (F)?**
   a Edward is David's father.
   b Sandra is Camilla's aunt.
   c Edward and Alexandra have a daughter.
   d Peter and Camilla have cousins.
   e David has two brothers.
   f Peter and Camilla's grandfather is Ann.
   g Ann's husband is Richard.
   h David has a wife.
   i Camilla is Peter's sister.
   j David is an uncle.

3 **Look at the family tree and complete the sentences.**
   a David is Sandra's _____.
   b Ann is Richard's _____.
   c Edward is Peter and Camilla's _____.
   d Sandra is Edward's _____.
   e Richard is Camilla's _____.
   f Peter is Alexandra's _____.
   g Camilla is Sandra's _____.
   h Peter is Ann and Richard's _____.

4 **Order the words in a–e to make questions.**
   a your / what / full / name / is / ? /
   _____
   b from / you / where / are / ?
   _____
   c live / where / you / do / ?
   _____
   d city / you / like / this / do / ?
   _____
   e a / do / have / you / family / big / ?
   _____

5 **Make it personal** Answer the questions in 4.

6 **Write questions for these answers a–e.**
   a _____
   Her name is Mariana.
   b _____
   My sister lives in Bogotá.
   c _____
   Yes. She loves Bogotá.
   d _____
   That old man is my grandfather.
   e _____
   No, he isn't Chinese. He's Japanese.

2.4 When do you check your phone?

1 Read the information in the chart and complete the sentences with these words.

| always | never | occasionally | often | sometimes |

	Pedro	Ana	Luca	Sara	Jacob
check phone at breakfast	✓✓✓	✓✓✓✓	✓✓	✓	✓✓✓
text friends at school	✓	✓✓✓✓	✓✓	✓✓✓	✓
email homework to teacher	✓✓	✗	✓✓✓	✗	✓
take phone to the gym	✗	✓✓	✓	✓✓✓	✓✓✓✓
play games on phone	✓✓✓✓	✗	✓✓✓✓	✓✓	✓✓✓
watch movies on computer	✓	✓✓✓	✓✓	✓✓	✗
leave phone at home	✗	✗	✗	✓	✓✓

a Pedro ____always____ plays games on his phone.
b Sara _____ takes her phone to the gym.
c Jacob _____ emails his homework to his teacher.
d Luca and Sara _____ watch movies on the computer.
e Ana _____ texts her friends at school.
f Jacob _____ checks his phone at breakfast.
g Pedro, Ana, and Luca _____ leave their phones at home.

2 Use the information in the chart to write five different sentences about the teenagers.
   a _____
   b _____
   c _____
   d _____
   e _____

3 **Make it personal** Write sentences about how often you do these things.
   text your friends at school _____
   call your grandparents _____
   go to the gym _____
   play games on your phone _____

Connect
Use your questions to interview a classmate. Record their answers on your phone.

2.5 How do you celebrate your birthday?

1 **Add the missing word to questions a–g.**
   a How old are you?
   b Where you live?
   c you have a boyfriend / girlfriend?
   d What time you go to bed on weekdays?
   e Do you any brothers or sisters?
   f Do use the Internet?
   g What you do on the weekend?

2 **Make it personal** Write your personal answers to a–g in **1**.

3 **Order these words to make follow-up questions.**
   1 name / ? / is / what / his / her
   2 your / is / when / ? / birthday
   3 use / often / ? / you / do / it / how
   4 do / many / sleep / ? / you / how / hours
   5 weekdays / do / on / ? / you / what / do
   6 a / is / cool / ? / city / it
   7 old / are / how / they / ?

4 **Match follow-up questions 1–7 in 3 to a–g in 1.**

5 **Complete the adverbs with a, e, o, or u and number them in order of frequency, 1–6.**
   ☐ __lw__ys
   ☐ n__v__r
   ☐ __cc__si__n__lly
   ☐ __ft__n
   ☐ s__m__tim__s
   ☐ __s__ __lly

6 **Make it personal** Use the adverbs in **5** to make sentences a–i true for you.
   a I go to parties. *I sometimes go to parties.*
   b I go out on the weekend.
   c I go to a party for New Year's Eve.
   d I play soccer.
   e My mom talks on the phone when she drives.
   f My father prepares meals.
   g I study English at home.
   h I give my father a gift on Father's Day.
   i I get up early on the weekend.

7 ◯ 2.6 **Look at photos 1–6. What can you say in each situation? Listen to check.**
   a H_____ b_____!
   b H_____ N_____ Y_____!
   c Have a g_____ t_____!
   d M_____ C_____!
   e C_____!
   f Enjoy y_____ m_____!

Can you remember …
- 8 *go phrases* with places around town? SB→p. 18
- the days of the week? SB→p. 18
- how to tell the time? SB→p. 19
- 10 verbs for your morning routine? SB→p. 20
- words for family? SB→p. 22
- how to ask yes / no questions? SB→p. 23
- 6 verbs for your cell phone? SB→p. 25
- 6 frequency adverbs? SB→p. 25
- 6 phrases for special occasions? SB→p. 27

3

3.1 What's the weather like?

1 Match song lines a–f to pictures 1–6. Complete the song line with a weather word.

Some Famous Weather Songs

a "The ___fog___ is so thick, I can't see my hands."
  The Wallflowers
b "I'm singing in the _____. What a glorious feeling, I'm happy again." *Gene Kelly*
c "The answer, my friend, is blowing in the _____." *Bob Dylan*
d "Hey! You! Get off of my _____. Don't hang around 'cause two is a crowd." *Rolling Stones*
e "Here comes the _____, and I say it's alright." *The Beatles*
f "But as long as you love me so, let it _____, let it _____, let it _____." *Dean Martin*

2 ▶3.1 Make sentences about the weather. Follow the model.

Model: *Wow! Look at the sun.*
You: *Yeah, it is really sunny today.*

3 🔵 **Make it personal** Cross out one extra word in each question. Then, answer a–e.
a What's ~~it~~ the weather like today?
b Is it hot in out?
c What does is the weather usually like in your city?
d How is the weather in these days?
e Is it snowy in July in the your country?

4 ▶3.2 Listen and match these answers to the questions in **3**.
☐ It's usually very windy, but today it's calm.
☐ Yes, in some places. You need a warm jacket.
☐ It's really nice. Very warm and sunny, I love it.
☐ It's cold and rainy. Yuck.
☐ Yes, it is. It's 40 degrees. I hate it.

5 Choose the correct form.
a The weather in my city is really crazy. Sometimes it's **sun / sunny** but **cold / clouds** in the morning, but in the afternoon it's **warm / warming** and **rain / rainy**.
b I don't like **rain / rainy** days. I love **hot / hotty**, **sun / sunny** weather.
c I like to stay home and watch TV when it's **snow / snowing**. It's too **cold / cool** to be outdoors.
d My best friend prefers to go to the beach when it's **cloud / cloudy**. I think she's afraid of the **sun / sunny**.
e London is famous for its **fog / foggy**, but, in my opinion, it's more probable for a tourist to see **fog / foggy** days in San Francisco than in London.

3.2 Are you busy at the moment?

1 Maya is writing to her friend in Finland. Use the map to cross out the wrong answer in the first paragraph. Complete the months in the other paragraphs.

From: Maya
To: Heidi
Subject: My city!

Hi Heidi,
My name is Maya and I'm from Trinidad and Tobago, two **islands** / **mountains** in **the Mediterranean** / **the Caribbean**. Port-of-Spain, is **an island** / **the capital** and it's located in the **southeast** / **northwest** of Trinidad, the **big** / **small** island. I live there!
There are only two seasons here. The dry season starts in J__u__r__ and ends in J__n__ and the wet season goes from J__l__ to D__c____b__r. If you like hot weather and nice beaches, this is the perfect place for a vacation. It's never cold here. The temperatures in the rainy season are similar to the temperatures when it's sunny and dry. The only bad thing about our weather is the wind. Sometimes, it's very strong!
Anyway, the best time to visit is during Carnival, in F__b__u____y or M_____h! Our Carnival is famous. We dance to calypso or soca, our local music. You have to see it. It's just wonderful!
Email me, please. I want to know more about you and your city.

Maya

2 Reread the email. True (T) or False (F)?
a Maya lives in the Caribbean.
b Port-of-Spain is only the capital of Trinidad.
c Trinidad is to the south of Tobago.
d There is no winter in Maya's country.
e Winds are cold in Trinidad and Tobago.
f Carnival is in the rainy season.

3 Complete the reply with the present continuous form of the verbs in parentheses.

From: Heidi
To: Maya
Subject: Re: My city!

Hi Maya,
I live in Kokkola, a small town in Finland. Winter _____ (**start**) here and it's very cold. Daytime _____ (**get**) shorter and nights _____ (**become**) longer. Right now my brother _____ (**do**) his homework and my mom _____ (**buy**) groceries at the store.
I _____ (**write**) to you on his laptop, so I don't have a lot of time. Talk to you later, OK?
Best,
Heidi

4 ▶3.3 Choose the correct phone phrases to complete dialogues 1–4. There are two extra phrases. Listen to check.

No problem.	I can't hear you.
Are you busy?	Don't worry.
The line's busy.	My battery's dying.
Call you later.	Sorry, wrong number.

1 A _____?
  B Sorry, yes. I'm at work.
  A OK, _____.
2 A Hi. Do you want to meet me at 8?
  B Can you repeat that? Sorry? _____.
  A _____. I said, "Do you want to meet me at 8?"
3 A Hello?
  B Is this Hannah?
  A Uh, no.
  B _____.
4 A Call Mike now.
  B I am calling him. _____.

3.3 What are you doing these days?

1 Match dialogues 1–6 to photos a–f.

1 A Is Dad making lunch? I'm hungry.
  B Yes, he his.
2 A Where's Maria?
  B She's driving to see her grandmother in hospital.
3 A Is that Jordan walking across the street?
  B Yes, and he's listening to music on his phone again.
4 A What are they doing now?
  B They're playing video games.
5 A Where's your sister working these days?
  B She's a nurse in our local hospital.
6 A Hurry up! What are you doing?
  B We're eating our breakfast.

2 Order the words to make questions. Then write answers in the present continuous using the words in parentheses.
  a your / sleeping / is / mom ?
    _No,_ _____ (working)
  b doing / you / the kitchen / are / in / what ?
    _____ (make cookies)
  c he / where / these days / is / living ?
    _____ (Mexico City)
  d with / is / dancing / who / brother / your ?
    _____ (his girlfriend)
  e playing / are / tennis / they ?
    _____ (basketball)
  f what / you / drinking / now / are ?
    _____ (a cup of coffee)

3 ▶3.4 Make sentences about the photos. Follow the model.
Model: *Photo 1. What's she doing?*
You: *She's reading the newspaper.*

4 Match what each speaker says to one of these problems.

consumerism   identity theft   Internet addiction
         isolation   violence

a *My little brother is always sitting in his room playing video games and doesn't have any friends.*
  _____

b *I think our city is very bad now. My grandparents won't go out at night because of all the fighting.*
  _____

c *My sisters are always at the shopping mall buying new things. I don't understand it – why do they want so many clothes and shoes?*
  _____

d *I don't like using my computer for banking. I don't want people to take my personal information and get my money.*
  _____

e *Some people are on their computers for 20 hours a day. They are playing games, shopping, or reading the news.*
  _____

3.4 What do you do after school / work?

1 Answer the questions about these celebrities.
Who is this?
What does he / she do?
What is he / she doing now?

| actor | athlete | activist | singer |

a) Usain Bolt
This is Usain Bolt.
He _____
Now he _____

b) Emma Watson
_____
_____
_____

c) Drake
_____
_____
_____

d) Malala Yousafzai
_____
_____
_____

2 🔵 **Make it personal** Write about your own family.
My father is _____
He usually _____
At the moment he _____

3 ▶ 3.5 Complete dialogues 1–4. Choose the correct verb form. Listen to check.

1 A Hi! What **do you do / are you doing** here?
   B I'm just **drinking a coffee / drink a coffee** and **relax / relaxing** on my break.
   A I see. But, what **do you do / are you doing**?
   B I'm a teacher. I always **having a coffee / have a coffee** on my break.

2 A Excuse me. What is that? I mean, what kind of motorcycle **do you ride / are you riding**?
   B Today I **ride / am riding** a scooter, but I have two motorcycles. I usually **am riding / ride** my big Harley.
   A OK, thanks.

3 A So, what **are you reading / do you read**?
   B Oh, it's a story about Shakira and Piqué. They are …
   A No, I mean … What are you reading? You **aren't / don't** usually **reading / read** Hello!.
   B Oh! No, you're right. I usually **read / am reading** The New Yorker, but I … er … I **am liking / like** the pictures in this kind of magazine.

4 A Mom! Lucy and her friends **are watching / watch** a movie!
   B Yes, that's right. They **watch / are watching** Pitch Perfect.
   A But, Mom, it's 6 o'clock. I always **am watching / watch** Sunny Street at 6.
   B Well, you can miss one day. The story is always the same, anyway.

4 Complete with the present continuous or simple present of the verbs in parentheses.

.... **Are BASE jumpers crazy?** ....

Jack Agnello and Logan Reed _____ (**be**) BASE jumpers. They _____ (**jump**) from buildings, antennas, bridges, and mountains and they _____ (**use**) parachutes to land safely. At the moment, they _____ (**plan**) their next jump. They _____ (**want**) to jump from a bridge in West Virginia, but they _____ (**need**) to get permission to do it, so Logan _____ (**fill**) out a form at the moment while Jack _____ (**check**) the West Virginia BASE website to get more information. They are very excited about it!

3.5 Why are you learning English?

1 Complete these forum replies with **have to** or **want to**.

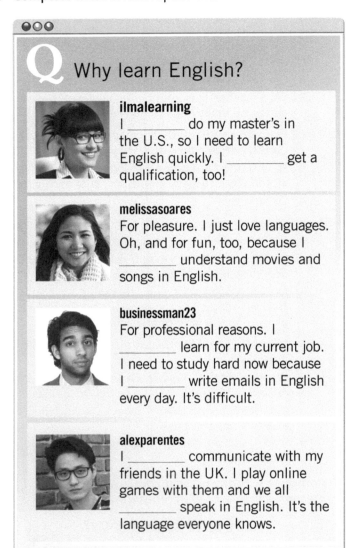

2 ▶ 3.6 Listen to the interview and write the letter of activities, a–f, according to what you hear.
 a get up early
 b be at the station at 6:30
 c work on weekends
 d prepare the evening presentation
 e change jobs
 f get married and have kids

	want to		have to	
	+	–	+	–
Taylor				
Josh and Isobel				
Serena				

3 ▶ 3.6 Listen again and answer the questions.
 a What does Taylor do?

 b What does Serena do?

 c What do Josh and Isobel do?

 d What does Serena want to be in the future?

4 **Make it personal** Write one or two sentences about why you are learning English. Use **want to** and **have to**.

5 ▶ 3.7 Sarah is taking care of her son, Philip. Listen to check the symptoms.

 cold   hot   hungry   thirsty   tired

6 Order the words in a–g to make offers for Philip. Which ones are good ideas?
 a drink / you / ? / a / do / want / cold
 b hot / you / a / would / drink / ? / like
 c you / ? / do / a / sweater / want
 d at / would / to / today / ? / you / home / like / stay
 e out / ? / to / want / you / go / do
 f ? / sandwich / a / would / like / you
 g to / you / go / do / ? / to / want / hospital

Can you remember ...
- 6 weather words? SB→p. 32
- 4 temperature words? SB→p. 32
- 6 activities? SB→p. 34
- the 12 months? SB→p. 35
- 6 seasons? SB→p. 35
- 5 more activities? SB→p. 38
- 2 ways of offering? SB→p. 41

4.1 Do you like tennis?

1 Complete a–f with the sports for each ball. Then complete g and h to find two more sports.

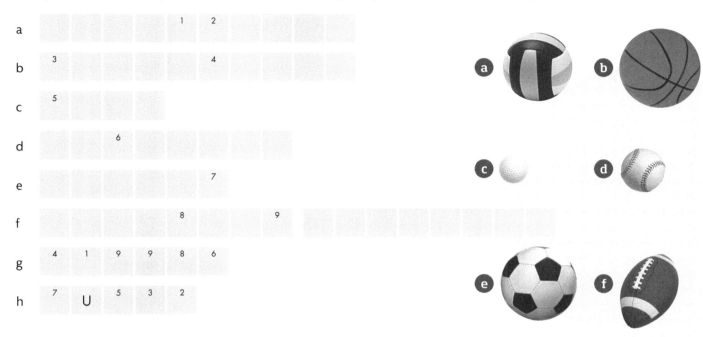

2 Circle the sport that is different and match it to the reason.
   a basketball, golf, soccer, rugby
   b golf, tennis, baseball, volleyball
   c cycling, swimming, surfing, windsurfing
   d soccer, swimming, cycling, running
   e skateboarding, golf, skiing, football

   ☐ You don't do it in water.
   ☐ You have to score points.
   ☐ You use your hands to hit the ball.
   ☐ You can only do it in winter.
   ☐ It isn't a team game.

3 ▶ 4.1 Listen to parents, Rob and Claire, talking about their children's sports. Complete the schedule with the sports. There are extra sports.

   ballet   baseball   basketball   soccer   swimming   tennis   volleyball

	Chloe	Randy
Monday		soccer
Tuesday		
Wednesday		
Thursday		
Friday		
Saturday		
Sunday		

4 ▶ 4.1 Listen again and answer the questions.
   a Who is practicing sports today?
   b What time does Chloe's swimming practice start?
   c What time does it finish?
   d Who has to take the children to volleyball practice?

5 ▶ 4.2 **Make it personal** Listen and say *I love / like / don't like / hate* + the sports. Follow the model.
   Model: *baseball*
   You: *I like baseball. / I don't like baseball.*

19

4.2 Can you drive a tractor?

1 Complete the groups with these words.

> a bus   a car   Chinese   Indian food   the drums   soccer
> French   Korean   the piano   pasta   a special meal   a tractor

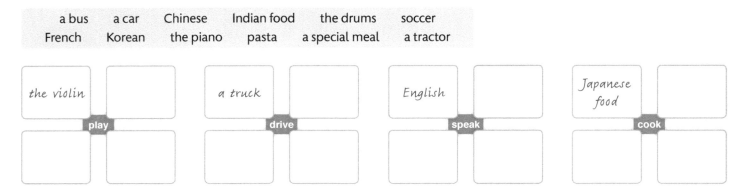

play	drive	speak	cook
the violin	a truck	English	Japanese food

2 Read the interview. Match questions a–d to the answers.

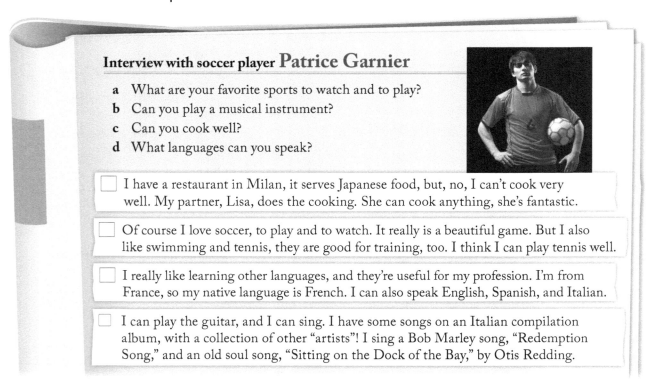

Interview with soccer player Patrice Garnier

a What are your favorite sports to watch and to play?
b Can you play a musical instrument?
c Can you cook well?
d What languages can you speak?

☐ I have a restaurant in Milan, it serves Japanese food, but, no, I can't cook very well. My partner, Lisa, does the cooking. She can cook anything, she's fantastic.

☐ Of course I love soccer, to play and to watch. It really is a beautiful game. But I also like swimming and tennis, they are good for training, too. I think I can play tennis well.

☐ I really like learning other languages, and they're useful for my profession. I'm from France, so my native language is French. I can also speak English, Spanish, and Italian.

☐ I can play the guitar, and I can sing. I have some songs on an Italian compilation album, with a collection of other "artists"! I sing a Bob Marley song, "Redemption Song," and an old soul song, "Sitting on the Dock of the Bay," by Otis Redding.

3 Reread. Answer questions a–d.
a Why does Patrice like tennis and swimming?
b Does Patrice sing original songs?
c Who prepares the food in Patrice's restaurant?
d How many languages can he speak?
e What two reasons does he give for learning languages?
f Why does he like watching soccer?

4 **Make it personal** Complete the box with a ✓ or ✗. Then write true sentences about you.

Activities	Can / Can't?
Play soccer	
Swim	
Cook a meal	
Ride a bicycle	
Drive a car	
Speak French	

I can _____
I can't _____

20

4.3 What languages can you speak?

1 Complete these song lines with **can** or **can't**. Do you know these songs?

a "I know I _____, I know I _____, be what I wanna be." **Nas**
b "Please _____ you, make this work for me?" **Sam Smith**
c "I _____ make you love me when you don't." **Adele**
d "You _____ remember my name." **Ed Sheeran**
e "I _____ live, if living is without you. I _____ give, I _____ give any more." **Mariah Carey**
f "_____ remember to forget you." **Shakira**
g "I _____ see you're sad, even when you smile, even when you laugh." **Eminem**
h "_____ you feel the love tonight?" **Elton John**

2 Write questions and answers about the people in the photos.

Jack

Chloe

Maria

a play / piano (✓)
   Can Jack play the piano?
   Yes, he can.

b cook? (✗)

c drive / car ? (✓)

Kyle

Sam

Amy

d play / violin? (✗)

e swim ? (✓)

f ski ? (✗)

3 ▶ 4.3 Ben can do everything well, but his brother Lance can't do anything very well! Make sentences about them. Follow the model.

Model: *Ben, bike*
You: *Ben can ride a bike very well.*
Model: *Lance, Japanese*
You: *Lance can't speak Japanese very well.*

4 **Make it personal** Make true sentences with **can** or **can't**. Add **very well**, or **at all** when necessary.

a I _____ use Google _____.
b I _____ understand directions _____.
c I _____ cook _____.
d I _____ remember names _____.
e I _____ use simple tools _____.
f I _____ speak two languages _____.
g I _____ bargain _____.
h I _____ make a good first impression.

21

4.4 Are you an organized person?

1 Look at the photo and answer questions a–i.
   a What's the young boy wearing?
   b How many people are wearing ties?
   c Are all of the people wearing shoes?
   d Are all of the women wearing belts?
   e Which person has a suit?
   f Who's wearing a skirt?
   g Are all of the men wearing shirts?
   h How many people are wearing shorts?
   i How many people are wearing a dress?

2 Write a description of one of these people and exchange it with a friend. Can you guess which person it is?

3 Order the clothes items to complete tweets a–e.

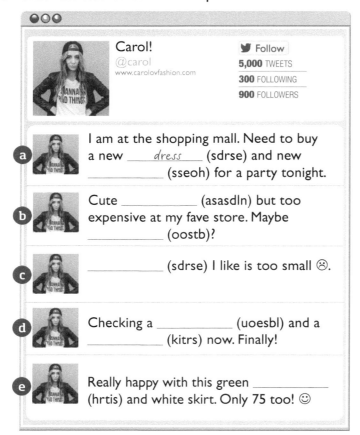

Carol!
@carol
www.carolovfashion.com
Follow
5,000 TWEETS
300 FOLLOWING
900 FOLLOWERS

a I am at the shopping mall. Need to buy a new ___dress___ (sdrse) and new _____ (sseoh) for a party tonight.

b Cute _____ (asasdln) but too expensive at my fave store. Maybe _____ (oostb)?

c _____ (sdrse) I like is too small ☹.

d Checking a _____ (uoesbl) and a _____ (kitrs) now. Finally!

e Really happy with this green _____ (hrtis) and white skirt. Only 75 too! ☺

4 Read the tweets and answer a–e.
   a What does she initially want to buy?
   b What do you think *fave* probably means?
   c What does she buy at the end?
   d How much do the clothes cost?
   e Do you know anyone like Carol?

5 Read the blog and complete it with:

's   hers   his   mine   ours
theirs   whose   yours

Which girl doesn't have a shoe collection? I know I do. _____ is 10 pairs, including shoes, boots, and sandals. How about _____? But _____ are small compared to some celebrities. My collection fills a closet, _____ fill entire rooms!

Khloe Kardashian has a huge closet. In fact it's the same size as two bedrooms! Khloe _____ closet is full of designer clothes, shoes, and bags and it is very well organized. All the shoes are organized by colors!

Poor Kendall Jenner says _____ is too small for all her clothes and it is very messy, so every two months she gives a lot of her unworn shoes and clothes to thrift stores. Then she can buy more designer goods to put back in the closet!

Even male celebrities like Mark Wahlberg have GIGANTIC shoe collections. _____ collection of 137 pairs of sneakers cost $100,000!

These celebrities have so many shoes I wonder if they ever ask "_____ shoes are these?"

6 ▶ 4.4 Ask questions using *whose*. Follow the model.

Model: *socks*
You: *Whose socks are these?*
Model: *sweater*
You: *Whose sweater is this?*

7 **Make it personal** Answer these questions about you.
   a How many pairs of shoes do you have?
   b How many pairs of jeans do you have?
   c What do you usually wear to work?
   d What do you wear to a wedding?

4.5 What shoe size are you?

1 Match a–e to the photos.
   a   credit card
   b   the fitting rooms
   c   contactless
   d   a receipt
   e   the store window

2 ▶ 4.5 Order these words to make a dialogue. Complete with words from **1**.

Salesclerk   you / can / ? / hi / help / I / ,
Jason   in / can / I / _____ / shorts / ? / hello / on / those / , / try
Salesclerk   are / here / , / you / sure / . there / _____ / over / are / .
Jason   great / are / they / ! I / ? / _____ / pay / by / can
Salesclerk   course / of / . it / is / _____ / ?
Jason   is / Yes / it / . ? / have / _____ / please / , / can / I

3 ▶ 4.6 Imagine you are at a store. The salesclerk shows you an item of clothing. Respond as in the examples. Follow the model.

Model: *brown coat*
You: *Can I try that brown coat on?*
Model: *blue jeans*
You: *Can I try those blue jeans on?*

4 ▶ 4.7 Listen to Katie and her boyfriend, Brian, in a shopping mall. Answer a–e.
   a   Does Brian like shopping?
      ☐ Yes, he does.
      ☐ No, he doesn't.
      ☐ He thinks it's OK.
   b   What kind of store are they in?
      ☐ A sports store.
      ☐ A clothes store.
      ☐ A shoe store.
   c   What size jeans does Brian need?
      ☐ S
      ☐ M
      ☐ L
   d   How much are the shorts?
      ☐ $16
      ☐ $46
      ☐ $60
   e   What does Katie buy in the end?
      ☐ Nothing.
      ☐ A blouse.
      ☐ A pair of shorts.

5 ▶ 4.8 Imagine you are shopping with Katie. Respond to the questions. Follow the model.

Model: *What do you think of these boots?*
You: *I like them. They look great.*
Model: *What do you think of this blouse?*
You: *I like it. It looks great.*

6 🎧 **Make it personal**   Tell your partner about the clothes and shoes you like wearing.

📶 Connect

Use the dialogue in **2** *to practice a similar one with your partner. Record your dialogue and send it to your teacher.*

Can you remember ...

▸ 7 sports?   SB→p. 44
▸ 10 activities?   SB→p. 46
▸ 10 abilities?   SB→p. 49
▸ 4 professions?   SB→p. 49
▸ 16 clothes items?   SB→p. 50
▸ 6 possessive pronouns?   SB→p. 51
▸ 4 clothes sizes?   SB→p. 53
▸ the place where you try on clothes?   SB→p. 53

5

5.1 Is there a mall in your area?

1 Complete the puzzle with places around town.

Across
1 You watch movies in a _____.
3 The Nile is a very long _____.
8 You buy books at a _____.
9 You can dance at a _____.

Down
2 You pay to swim in a _____.
3 Cars or horses compete at a _____.
4 You can have a picnic in a _____.
5 There are hundreds of stores at a _____.
6 You stay in a _____ when you go on vacation.
7 You take books from a _____ but only for a week or two.

2 ►5.1 Listen, mark the stress and the number of syllables in words a–h.

E.g.: ●○○ Syllable.

a bar
b club
c hotel
d museum
e park
f restaurant
g stadium
h theater

3 🗣 **Make it personal** Use the words in 1 and 2 to make true sentences for you.
a There's a fantastic _____ in my town.
b I think a _____ is an interesting place.
c There isn't a _____ near my house.
d There's a _____ near my house.
e There's more than one _____ in my town.
f My favorite _____ is called _____.

4 🗣 **Make it personal** Order the words to make sentences. Are they true for your town?
a 's / downtown / museum / a / there / .
b no / are / theaters / movie / here / there / .
c big / there / any / parks / aren't / .
d some / good / restaurants / are / there / .
e a / bookstore / 's / fantastic / there / .
f there / small / are / rivers / two / .

5 Complete the song lines with **there is**, (or **there's**) **there are**, **is there**, or **are there**.

a "Imagine _____ no heaven."
John Lennon

b "When I see your face, _____ not a thing that I would change." Bruno Mars

c "_____ nothin' you can't do now you're in New York." Alicia Keys

d "_____ many things that I would like to say to you, but I don't know how." Oasis

e "_____ a lady who's sure all that glitters is gold, and she's buying a stairway to heaven."
Led Zeppelin

f "_____ anybody going to listen to my story?"
The Beatles

g "_____ a chance for me?" Frank Sinatra

h "And though _____ times when I hate you"
Beyoncé

i "_____ any more real cowboys?" Neil Young

🔊 Connect

Try to find these songs online. What's your favorite one?

5.2 What are your likes and dislikes?

1 ▶5.2 Guess which of the phrases below complete crazy statistics a–h. Listen to check.

cleaning the house   cooking   eating out   exercising
going out   playing video games   shopping   watching TV

What a life !
Where does all our time go? Look at these crazy statistics.

a American men spend about 3 hours a week _____.
b On average, French people spend 32 minutes a day _____.
c Americans spend approximately 50 minutes a day _____.
d 58% of Americans like _____ once a week.
e On average, American men spend 13.3 hours a week _____.
f Only 53% of British teenagers like _____ on weekends.
g Americans spend about 98 hours a month _____.
h American teens spend about 1 hour a day _____.

2 ▶5.3 Express your emotions! Follow the model.
Model: *cleaning the house. Sad!*
You: *I hate cleaning the house!*
Model: *watching TV. OK.*
You: *I don't mind watching TV.*
Model: *eating out. Happy!*
You: *I love eating out.*

3 ▶5.4 Listen to Leo and Becky talking about the statistics in **1**. Which activity do they both like?

4 Complete the labels with these verbs and match them to photos a–f.

Clean   Do   Play   Tidy   Wash   Watch

☐ _____ the laundry.
☐ _____ my bedroom.
☐ _____ a movie.
☐ _____ the dishes.
☐ _____ video games.
☐ _____ the bathroom.

5 Read the extract and answer a and b.
a Where is the extract from?
☐ A book.
☐ A newspaper.
☐ A poster.
b The extract is ...
☐ selling a product.
☐ for fun.
☐ giving information.

6 ▶5.5 Listen and complete a–h with the correct form of the verbs.

TV! week | **Modern Families. 8:45 p.m. Channel 5**
Recent statistics show that parents do most of the housework, around 9 hours a week compared to teenagers' 4.9 hours. In this episode, the team is talking to Celia Monroe, 49, and her son, Angelo, 15, about how this affects their lives and their free time.

a Angelo _____ doing his laundry.
b Angelo absolutely _____ washing the dishes.

hate (x2)   have   like (x2)   love (x2)
mind (x2)   clean

c He never _____ his room.
d He _____ playing video games and watching movies.
e Celia _____ doing the chores.
f Celia _____ washing the dishes.
g She _____ cleaning the bathroom.
h She _____ time for free time activities.
i She _____ to swim when she can.
j She _____ to read novels.

🔊 Connect
Use your phone to record yourself talking about your likes and dislikes.

25

5.3 What do you like doing on vacation?

1 Read the article about the Galápagos islands and match the highlighted words to the photos.

There are over 50 islands in the Galápagos archipelago, and there are many ways to explore them. Snorkeling. Biking. Walking. Kayaking. Just select the option for you, or try all of them in our exclusive vacation package!
What to do: There are thousands of unique birds and animals here, and you can come face-to-face with wonderful wildlife. Swim with penguins on Bartolomé island. Go snorkeling on Floreana and see the turtles or the pink flamingoes in the lagoons. See sea lions on the white sand beaches of San Cristóbal, or travel to the quiet forests of the island to find the giant tortoises.

2 ▶5.6 Reread and answer a–d. Listen to check.
 a What three activities can you do in the sea?
 b Do you have to choose **one** way to explore the islands?
 c Do tortoises live in the sea?
 d Find five examples of wildlife.

3 What do Katy, Sara, and Tom like doing on vacation? Choose the best three activities for each person.

snorkeling   sightseeing   sunbathing   camping   kayaking   swimming   reading novels
   visiting museums   eating out

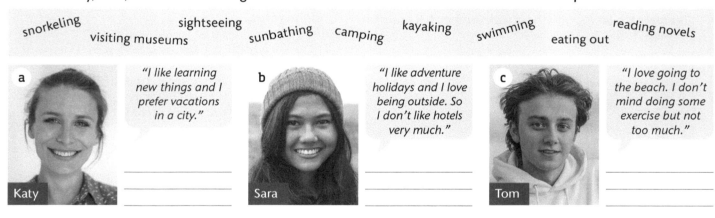

a Katy: "I like learning new things and I prefer vacations in a city."

b Sara: "I like adventure holidays and I love being outside. So I don't like hotels very much."

c Tom: "I love going to the beach. I don't mind doing some exercise but not too much."

4 **Make it personal** Complete the puzzle with vacation activities. For example, ☠ = N. Check the ones that you like doing.

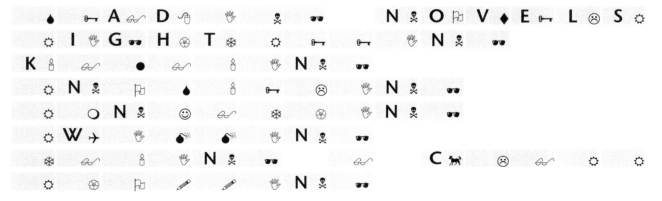

26

5.4 How often do you leave voice messages?

1 ▶5.7 Complete the blog with the correct form of these words. Listen to check.

check   close   feed   give   let   open   pick   put   take (x2)   wash   water

Beth's Blog

Hi everyone! Here I am in the beautiful city of Bath. I've got a new job for the summer – I'm a house sitter. The family are in New York on holiday and I'm _____ care of their house, garden, two dogs, one cat, and lots of fish!

It's a big house with a garden and I have a list of chores I have to do every day. Most of them are fun and I don't mind doing them, but I don't like _____ the plants. They have lots and lots of plants!!

It's very hot here this summer, so every morning I _____ the windows and doors and _____ the cat out. He usually sleeps under a tree all day. Then I _____ the dogs, Toby and Freddie, and _____ the fish some food – they have 8 beautiful fish. I _____ there is some clean water for the cat, and after breakfast I _____ the dogs for a long walk. They love going to the park and swimming in the lake there.

When I get home, I _____ up the mail and _____ it on the table in the kitchen. I spend most of the day reading or sunbathing in the garden. Sometimes I go sightseeing in Bath. It's brilliant!

In the evening I _____ the windows, _____ the dishes, and go to bed. I don't get paid for this job, but I love being a house sitter.

2 Read the blog again and answer a–c.
a Where is Beth living now?
b What does the cat like doing?
c How much money does Beth get every week?

3 ▶5.8 Listen to four phone messages. Check ✓ (do) or cross ✗ (don't do) the activities.
a Water the plants.   Feed the cat.   Close the windows.
b Cook dinner.   Prepare a salad.   Wash the dishes.
c Take the dog for a walk.   Feed the dog.   Feed the cat.
d Buy some herbal tea.   Clean the house today.   Go to the grocery store.

4 Complete instructions a–e.

a _____ the windows in the morning and close _____ again at _____. Thanks.

b Remember to phone Mom and sing _____ "Happy Birthday." XXX

c After dinner, _____ forget to wash the _____ and dry _____ !!!

d Your brother wants you to call _____ after 7 p.m.

e Buy some coffee and leave _____ on the kitchen table. Thanks.

5.5 Do you live near here?

1 ▶5.9 Complete a–e with these adjectives. Listen to check.

> boring   cheap   messy   near   safe

a It's not dangerous to swim here—it's _____. Look! There are a lot of people swimming.
b What do you mean it's expensive? It's only $80. That's very _____ for a tablet.
c My office is very tidy. I hate _____ rooms.
d I like history, it's really interesting. But I always sleep in my math class. It's so _____.
e I live quite far from downtown, but there's a good shopping mall _____ my house.

2 Read this magazine article. True (T) or False (F)?

Camping – but not as you know it!

Do you think that camping equals cold, rain, insects in your clothes, and no showers? Do you think that camping is cheap but messy? Not anymore. "Glamping" is the new craze in vacations—you stay in a tent, but it's a five-star tent. Camping with glamour! If you want to go glamping here are some tips:

- Search the Internet for a good price. It can be expensive!
- Remember to take stylish but warm clothes. You want to look good, not blue with cold!
- Recharge your phone before you go. There isn't always electricity on campgrounds, even glamorous ones!
- Take an umbrella. You can't change the weather and you don't want your hair to get wet!

a Camping is always messy.
b "Glamping" is a recent idea.
c Glamping usually costs more than camping.
d You can always watch TV when glamping.

3 Match new words 1–4 to definitions a–d.

1 a **gray**cation
2 info**tain**ment
3 **net**iquette
4 a **scree**nager

a being polite on the Internet
b a young person that watches TV, plays video games and uses the Internet all the time
c a TV show that mixes facts with fun
d staying with your grandparents to save money

4 ▶5.10 Listen and mark these buildings on the map.

> bookstore   club   gym
> ID English   museum

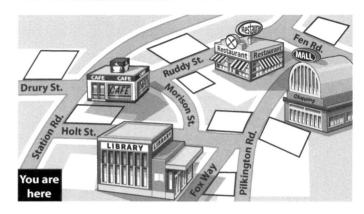

5 ▶5.11 Ask for directions. Follow the model.

Model: *Do you know. Library?*
You: *Do you know where the library is?*
Model: *Mall. Near here?*
You: *Is there a mall near here?*

6 ▶5.12 Answer the questions. Follow the model.

Model: *Is there a café near here?*
You: *Yeah, there's one on Station Road.*

7 🙂 **Make it personal** Write directions from school to your favorite place in your city.

> Leave school and turn …

Can you remember …

▸ 16 places around town? SB→p.58
▸ how to describe your town? SB→p.59
▸ 10 things you do in your free time? SB→p.60
▸ 4 verbs to talk about what you prefer to do? SB→p.60
▸ 14 vacation activities? SB→p.62
▸ how to leave a message telling someone what to do? SB→p.64
▸ 9 adjectives? SB→p.66
▸ 2 new English words for vacations? SB→p.66
▸ how to ask for directions? SB→p.67

Audio Script

Unit 1

1.1
Countries
Australia – Australian
Brazil – Brazilian
Canada – Canadian
Chile – Chilean
India – Indian
Korea – Korean
Continents
Africa – African
America – American
Asia – Asian
Europe – European

1.3
HBO
CNN
ABC
BBC
MTV
VH1
ESPN
NBC

1.6
1 The total is thirty euros.
2 Here's your ticket and twenty-five dollars.
3 That's two dollars. There you go. Enjoy!
4 That's forty-eight dollars! That's ridiculous!

1.7
C = Cynthia   G = Geoffrey

C Hello, tourist information, this is Cynthia. What can I do for you today?
G Yes, can you help me, please?
C Sure, no problem. I just need some information from you. What's your name?
G Geoffrey Jenkins. That's G-E-O-double-F-R-E-Y. Jenkins, J-E-N-K-I-N-S.
C Thank you. And what is your nationality?
G I'm American
C And what's your hotel address, Mr. Jenkins?
G Hotel Panorama. 63 Sea Parade.
C Thank you. And what's your telephone number?
G My cell number is 860-4279.
C Thanks. And, uh, what's your email address?
G It's gjenkins90@ncfc.com.
C gjenkins19? One nine?
G No, 90, nine zero.
C Ok, thanks. Now what do you want to know?

1.11
What's your first name?
What's your last name?
Where are you from?
What's your nationality?
What's your address?
How old are you?

1.12
a How are you?
b What's new?
c See you later.
d Thank you!
e What's up?
f I don't understand.

Unit 2

2.2
W = woman   M = man

a W Excuse me. What time is it, please?
  M It's six forty-five.
b M Excuse me. Excuse me. What time is it?
  W Uh ... It's about half past seven.
  M Oh, my train!
c W Psst! Is it time to go home yet?
  M No, it's only four o'clock.
d M What time is it?
  W It's twelve forty-five. Time for lunch!
e M Is it two forty-five yet?
  W No! It's a quarter past three.
  M What? Wow, I'm really late.

2.5
I = interviewer   D = David

I Hello, please introduce yourself and tell us a bit about your family.
D Ok ... My name is David and I have two siblings, Edward and Sandra. Our parents are Richard and Ann. Hmm ... Edward lives with his wife, Alexandra, and their children, Peter and Camilla.

2.6
W = woman   M = man   G = girl

a W Hey! There you are! So, how old are you now?
  M Uh ... twenty-one.
  W Haha! You always say that! Here's your gift. Happy birthday!
b M Look! It's eleven fifty-nine ... quick everybody. Get a drink!
  All 10, 9, 8, 7, 6, 5, 4, 3, 2, 1 ... Happy New Year!
  M Happy New Year!
c W Do you have everything?
  G Yes, Mom.
  W Do you have your passport?
  G Yes, Mom.
  W OK, darling. Have a good trip!
  G OK. See you soon.
d All Jingle bells, jingle bells, jingle all the way. Hey! Merry Christmas!
  W Merry Christmas!
e W I love weddings and you look fantastic! Congratulations!
f G Hmmmmm. That smells delicious!
  M Thank you. We have chicken and vegetables to start and then fruit salad. Enjoy your meal.

Unit 3

3.2
W = woman   M = man   G = girl

a W What is the weather like today?
  G It's really nice. Very warm and sunny, I love it!
b W Is it hot out?
  M Yes, it is. It's 40 degrees! I hate it.
c W1 What is the weather usually like in your city?
  W2 It's usually very windy, but today it's calm.
d M1 How is the weather these days?
  M2 It's cold and rainy. Yuck!
e W Is it snowy in July in your country?
  M Yes, in some places. You need a warm jacket!

Audio Script

3.6

R = Rita　T = Taylor　S = Selena
J = Josh　I = Isobel

R This evening in *Job Corner* we have four different professionals. First let's meet Taylor Gregor. Hi, Taylor.
T Hi, Rita.
R So tell us, Taylor, what do you do?
T I'm a web designer.
R Tell us about your routine. Do you have to get up early every morning?
T No, I don't have to get up early at all. I make my own hours.
S Well, my name is Serena James, and I'm a police officer.
R Do you have a fixed schedule?
S Yes, I have to be at the station at six thirty every morning. Sometimes I need to work weekends, too.
R I see. I want to ask Josh and Isobel the same question. Please tell our listeners what you do.
J Well, we are Josh and Isobel Markham and we work together.
R What do you do?
I Josh and I are singers. We sing at nightclubs.
R So you have free mornings and afternoons?
J No, we don't. We have to work in the afternoon to prepare for the evening presentation.
R Are you all happy with your jobs?
J/I Yeah, sure, yes.
T I think so, yes. I have a lot of freedom and I use my creativity every day.
R How about you, Serena?
S To be honest, I want to change jobs. The work in the police force is very hard, and I want to get married and have kids. So I want to go back to college and become a teacher. They have long vacations.
R OK, it's time for our break. More from our guests after these messages …

3.7

P = Philip　S = Sarah

P Mom! I feel bad. My stomach and, and my head.
S Oh, baby! What's the matter? Are you OK?
P No, Mom. I'm not. I feel really bad. I feel …
S What is it? Do you have a fever? Are you hot?
P Oh, yes, yes. And then sometimes I'm very cold.
S Oh, baby! Are you hungry?
P No, no. I'm not hungry. But I'm very thirsty. And I feel tired.

Unit 4

4.1

R = Rob　C = Claire

R Claire, what time does Randy have soccer practice today?
C Oh, Rob! He only has soccer practice on Monday. Today is Tuesday.
R Oh, right, sorry. So today Chloe has her …
C Swimming class. Yes, at four thirty.
R So what is Randy doing today?
C Rob, please! Look at the schedule! He has soccer on Monday and tennis practice on Thursday. Chloe swims on Tuesday and has ballet classes on Friday afternoon. What kind of father are you?
R The kind that has a terrible memory?
C Well, Chloe finishes at six thirty today. Don't forget that! And you have to take them both to volleyball on Saturday.

4.7

K = Katie　B = Brian
S1 = salesperson 1　S2 = salesperson 2

K Oh, Brian! Can we go in here?
B Oh, Katie! Not again! How many stores do we have to go to?
K Oh, come on, Brian. This is the last one. I promise.
B Come on then, let's go.
K Great!

K Hey, Brian, what do you think of this blouse?
B It's … uh … It's interesting.
K Look, Brian. I need to do some shopping and you are not helping. You need some new jeans. Why don't you go and try some on? See you later.
B Fine. See you later.

S1 Hi. Do you need any help?
B Yes, I, uh … can I try those jeans on, please?
S1 Sure. What size?
B Uh … medium … I think.
S1 Medium? Here you are. The fitting rooms are over there.
B Thank you.

B Uh … excuse me … can I get these in a large, please?
S1 Of course, sir. Here you are.

B Hi, Katie. So, these are my new jeans. What do you think?
K They look great, Brian. Really good.
B What are you getting?
K Well, I have these shorts and uh … this blouse.
B Oh. The … blouse.
K What?
B Well … it's just … it's the color. Orange and … and pink … and …
S2 Next, please! Hello, ma'am. Shorts and a blouse. That's …
K No, no. Not the blouse. Er … Only the shorts, please.
S2 OK. That's $60, please.
K How much? Uh … I … No. No, thank you. Come on, Brian, let's go.

Unit 5

5.4

B = Becky　L = Leo

B Hey, Leo. Look at these statistics! They are crazy!
L I don't know, Becky. Only one hour a day playing video games. I love video games. I play for two hours a day easily.
B Really! Ugh, video games! I hate them. They are so boring!
L OK, well, what about you? What do you like doing?
B Well, I like going out with friends, you know, socializing. Not just sitting at home playing video games all the time.
L Hey! I like to go out, too! I just don't like shopping. That's what you do all the time.
B Ugh! No way! I don't like shopping either. I don't mind shopping malls, because I love to watch movies …

55

Audio Script

L Ha! So you love to sit in the movie theater watching movies and I love to sit in my room playing video games.

▶ 5.5

I = interviewer   C = Celia

I So, Celia, tell me about Angelo. Does he help you around the house?
C Well, he's not too bad, I mean, he doesn't mind doing his laundry—not the laundry, just his. But he absolutely hates washing the dishes and he never cleans his room—it's chaos in there!
I And what does he do in his free time?
C Oh, he's in his bedroom a lot. He loves playing video games and watching movies. All the time.
I What about you? Do you like doing the chores?
C No, I don't! I guess Angelo is like me! Hmm … I guess I don't mind washing the dishes because I know I can do it correctly. I hate cleaning the bathroom, but I have to do it.
I And how about your free time?
C Free time! You're joking! Hmm … I love to swim when I can, and I like to read novels, too. But I don't really have time for anything like that.

▶ 5.6

a You can snorkel, kayak or swim.
b No, you don't. There are many ways to explore them.
c No, they don't. They live on land, in the forests.
d The five examples of wildlife are penguins, turtles, flamingoes, sea lions, and tortoises.

▶ 5.7

B = Beth

B: Hi, everyone! Here I am in the beautiful city of Bath. I've got a new job for the summer – I'm a house sitter. The family are in New York on holiday and I'm taking care of their house, garden, two dogs, one cat, and lots of fish!
It's a big house with a garden, and I have a list of chores I have to do every day. Most of them are fun and I don't mind doing them, but I don't like watering the plants. They have lots and lots of plants!! It's very hot here this summer, so every morning I open the windows and doors and let the cat out. He usually sleeps under a tree all day. Then I feed the dogs, Toby and Freddie, and give the fish some food – they have 8 beautiful fish. I check there is some clean water for the cat, and after breakfast I take the dogs for a long walk. They love going to the park and swimming in the lake there.
When I get home, I pick up the mail and put it on the table in the kitchen I spend most of the day reading or sunbathing in the garden. Sometimes I go sightseeing in Bath. It's brilliant! In the evening I close the windows, wash the dishes, and go to bed.
I don't get paid for this job, but I love being a house sitter.

▶ 5.8

a Hi, Martin, can you water the plants and feed the cat? Oh, and please don't close the windows. Don't worry, the cat can't escape, she's too fat.
b Hi, Tim, I'm working late today. Please cook dinner and prepare a salad. Don't wash the dishes. I can do them after dinner. Bye for now.
c Hi, it's me again. Don't walk the dog, he has a bad foot. But don't forget to feed him. See you later.
d Hi, darling. There's no herbal tea in the kitchen. Can you go to the grocery store and buy some, please? Love you.

▶ 5.10

M = man   W = woman   G = girl
B = boy

a M Is there a museum near here?
  W Yes, it's about five minutes from here. Go straight along Station Road and turn left on Drury Street, it's on your right. It's very big, you can't miss it.
  M Thanks.
b G Is there a bookstore near here?
  M Yeah, it's there, on the corner of Station Road and Holt Street.
  G Oh, yes, thank you.
c B Do you know where the ID English school is?
  W Hmm … I think you have to turn right on Holt Street and then right again after the library. The school is on that street.
d M1 Are there any clubs in this town?
  M2 Yeah, there's one near Luigi's. Go straight on Station Road and take the second right. Then turn left on Ruddy Street. The club is on the left, opposite the restaurant.
e W Where is a good place to exercise here?
  M There is a gym near the mall. Go to the end of Holt Street and turn left on Pilkington Road. The gym is the first building on your right.

Answer Key

Unit 1

1.1
1 **Countries**
Australia, Brazil, Canada, Chile, India, Korea
Continents
Africa, America, Asia, Europe
2 Australian, Brazilian, Canadian, Chilean, Indian, Korean, African, American, Asian, European
3 b Indian c Chinese d Korea e Peruvian
4 1 B 's / Australian
   2 A Are   B 'm not / Korean
   3 A Is / Peruvian   B Indian / 's
   4 A American   B they're not / 're British
   5 A Mexican   B isn't / 's / Spanish
5 b ✓
   c My brother is a horrible singer.
   d You are an excellent actor.
   e ✓
   f I
6 a I think Star Wars is a terrible movie.
   b Luis Suárez is an excellent player.
   c I think São Paulo is a great city.
   d I think India is an interesting country.
   e Chris Pratt is a cool actor.
7 Personal answers.

1.2
1 a HBO b CNN c ABC d BBC e MTV f VH1 g ESPN h NBC
2 b go c a name d ten e eight f six g one
3 f hi – five
   c a guitar – a party
   g no – a nose
   b blue – you
   a a name – Spain
   e ten – yes
4 one, two, three, four, five, six, seven, eight, nine, ten
5 1 $16 / $14 2 $75 / $100 3 $20 / $10 4 $12 / $4
6 1 30 2 25 3 2 4 48
7 Hi! Nice to meet you. My first name's _____ and my last name's _____. I'm _____. I'm from _____. I'm _____.

1.3
1 First name: Geoffrey
   Last name: Jenkins
   Hotel address: Hotel Panorama, 63 Sea Parade.
   Phone: 860-4279
   Email: gjenkins90@nfc.com
3 a What's your (full) name?
   b Where do you live?
   c What's your cell phone / phone number?
   d What's your address?
   e What's your email address?
4 Personal answers.
5 laptop, key, sandwich, glasses, phone, lipstick
6

+ S	+ ES	-Y + IES
backpacks	addresses	cities
earrings	glasses	countries
keys	sandwiches	nationalities
phones		

7 1 This 2 That 3 These / them 4 those / They 5 These / They

1.4
1 our, his, your, their
2 a her his b her your c his her d ours our e they're their f yours your
3 a The White House b The Pink House c Shakira d Levi's e Snoopy f Purple g Red and yellow h Nemo i An apple j Charlie Brown k "Where is the love?"

1.5
1 1 American 2 Jamaica 3 08/31/90 4 Patel 5 23 6 45 Colt Street, Dallas, Texas
2 Personal answers.
3 a 1 Fine, thanks. b 2 Not much.
   c 1 Bye, for now. d 2 You're welcome.
   e 2 Nothing much. f 1 Oh, sorry.
4 Personal answers.

Unit 2

2.1
1 a to a b to the c to the d to a / the /to e - f to g to
3 a Sunday b Wednesday c Friday d Monday e Tuesday f Thursday g Saturday
4 a 4 b Saturn c Friday
5 b 7:30 c 4:00 d 12:45 e 3:15
6 a It's six fifteen b It's half past six.
   c It's five o'clock. d It's twelve fifteen.
   e It's two forty-five.
7 a What time do you go to school? b What time do you go to bed? c What time do you go to work? d What time do you get home? e What time do you get up? f What time do you go to the gym?
8 Personal answers.

2.2
1 b get dressed / up c get up / dressed d have breakfast e leave home f make the bed g take a shower h wake up
2 Personal answers.
3 at six thirty, immediately, for around, for twenty minutes, at around
4 a F b T c T d T e F f T
5 Personal answers.
6 A love B loves C loves D don't love E love F love / love / loves G love H doesn't love

2.3
1 David's family tree
   a Richard   e Alexandra
   b Ann   f Camilla
   c Sandra   g Peter
   d Edward
2 a F b T c T d F e F f F g T h F i T j T
3 a brother b wife c father d sister e grandfather f son g niece h grandson
4 a What is your full name? b Where are you from? c Where do you live? d Do you like this city? e Do you have a big family?
5 Personal answers.
6 (Possible answers)
   a What's her name?
   b Where does she / your sister live?
   c Does she like Bogotá?
   d Who is that old man?
   e Is he Chinese?

2.4
1 b often c occasionally d sometimes e always f often g never
2 Personal answers.
3 Personal answers.

2.5
1 b Where do you live? c Do you have a boyfriend / girlfriend? d What time do you go to bed on weekdays? e Do you have any brothers or sisters? f Do you use the Internet? g What do you do on the weekend?
2 Personal answers.
3 1 What is his / her name? 2 When is your birthday? 3 How often do you use it? 4 How many hours do you sleep? 5 What do you do on weekdays? 6 Is it a cool city? 7 How old are they?
4 a 2 b 6 c 1 d 4 e 7 f 3 g 5
5 1 always 6 never 5 occasionally 3 often 4 sometimes 2 usually
6 Personal answers.
7 a Happy birthday! d Merry Christmas!
   b Happy New Year! e Congratulations!
   c Have a good trip! f Enjoy your meal!

Unit 3

3.1
1 b rain c wind d cloud e sun f snow, snow, snow
   Pictures: 1e, 2d, 3a, 4f, 5b, 6c
3 b in c does d in e the
4 c, e, a, d, b
5 a sunny, cold, warm, rainy b rainy, hot, sunny c snowing, cold d cloudy, sun e fog, foggy

3.2
1 islands, the Caribbean, the capital, northwest, big, January, June, July, December, February, March
2 a T b F c T d T e F f F
3 is starting, is getting, are becoming, is doing, is buying, am writing
4 1 Are you busy / Call you later 2 I can't hear you / No problem 3 Sorry, wrong number 4 The line's busy

3.3
1 1 c 2 d 3 f 4 a 5 b 6 e
2 a Is your mum sleeping? No, she's working.
   b What are you doing in the kitchen? I'm making cookies.
   c Where is he living these days? He's living in Mexico City.
   d Who is your brother dancing with? He's dancing with his girlfriend.
   e Are they playing tennis? No, they're playing basketball.
   f What are you drinking now? I'm drinking a cup of coffee.
3 (Possible answers)
   2 He's cooking. / He's making lunch.
   3 She's drinking a cup of coffee.
   4 He's riding a motorcycle.
   5 They're watching TV.
   6 He's eating breakfast.
4 a isolation b violence c consumerism d identity theft e Internet addiction

3.4
1 a He's an athlete. Now he's driving (a/his car).
   b This is Emma Watson. She's an actor. Now she's eating.
   c This is Drake. He's a singer. Now he's watching basketball.
   d This is Malala Yousafzai. She's an activist. Now she's reading.
2 Personal answers.
3 1 are you doing, drinking a coffee, relaxing, do you do, have a coffee
   2 are you riding, am riding, ride
   3 are you reading, don't, read, read, like
   4 are watching, are watching, watch,
4 are, jump, use, are planning, want, need, is filling, is checking

Answer Key

3.5
1 want to, have to, want to, have to, have to, want to, have to

2
	want to +	want to −	have to +	have to −
Taylor				a
Josh and Isobel			d	
Serena	e, f		b, c	

3 a He's a web designer. b She's a police officer.
  c They are singers. d She wants to be a teacher.
4 Personal answers.
5 hot, cold, thirsty, tired
6 a Do you want a cold drink? ✓
  b Would you like a hot drink? ✓
  c Do you want a sweater? ✓
  d Would you like to stay at home today? ✓
  e Do you want to go out? ✗
  f Would you like a sandwich? ✗
  g Do you want to go to hospital? ✓

Unit 4

4.1
1 a volleyball b basketball c golf d baseball
  e soccer f American football g tennis h rugby
2 a Golf. It isn't a team game.
  b Volleyball. You use your hands to hit the ball.
  c Cycling. You don't do it in water.
  d Soccer. You have to score points.
  e Skiing. You can only do it in winter.
3 Chloe: swimming on Tuesday, ballet on Friday, volleyball on Saturday
  Randy: soccer on Monday, tennis on Thursday, volleyball on Saturday
4 a Chloe b 4.30 c 6.30 d Rob (dad)
5 Personal answers.

4.2
1 Play: the drums, soccer, the piano
  Drive: a bus, a car, a tractor
  Speak: Chinese, French, Korean
  Cook: Indian food, pasta, a special meal
2 c, a, d, b
3 a Tennis and swimming are good for training.
  b No, he sings songs by Bob Marley and Otis Redding.
  c His partner, Lisa.
  d He speaks four languages.
  e He likes learning languages and they are useful for his profession.
  f He thinks it's a beautiful game.
4 Personal answers.

4.3
1 a can, can b can c can't d can't e Can't, can't, can't f Can't g can h Can
2 b Can Chloe cook? No, she can't.
  c Can Maria drive a car? Yes, she can.
  d Can Kyle play the violin? No, he can't.
  e Can Sam swim? Yes, he can.
  f Can Amy ski? No, she can't.
4 Personal answers.

4.4
1 a Jeans and a T-shirt. b One. c No, some are wearing just socks. d No, only two. e The first man from the right. f The young girl. g No, two are wearing T-shirts. h Only one. The third woman from the right. i None.
2 Personal answers.
3 a shoes b sandals / boots c dress d blouse / skirt e shirt
4 a A dress and some shoes. b Favorite. c A shirt and a skirt. d $75 e Personal answers.

5 Mine, yours, ours, theirs, 's, hers, His, Whose
7 Personal answers.

4.5
1 d, a, c, e, b
2 S Hi, can I help you?
  J Hello, can I try on those shorts in **the store window**?
  S Sure, here you are. **The fitting rooms** are over there.
  J They are great! Can I pay by **credit card**?
  S Of course. Is it **contactless**?
  J Yes it is. Can I have a **receipt**, please?
4 a No, he doesn't. b A clothes store. c L. d $60 e Nothing.
6 Personal answers.

Unit 5

5.1
1 Across: 1 movie theater 3 river 8 bookstore 9 club
  Down: 2 swimming pool 3 racetrack 4 park 5 mall 6 hotel 7 library
2 a● b● c○● d○●● e● f●○○ g●○○ h●○
3 Personal answers.
4 a There's a museum downtown. b There are no movie theaters here. c There aren't any big parks. d There are some good restaurants. e There's a fantastic bookstore. f There are two small rivers.
5 a there's b there's c There's d There are e There's f Is there g Is there h there are i Are there

5.2
1 a cleaning the house b shopping c cooking d eating out e exercising f going out g watching TV h playing video games
3 They both like going out.
4 a Clean the bathroom. b Play video games. c Wash the dishes. d Watch a movie. e Do the laundry. f Tidy the bedroom.
5 a A newspaper b giving information
6 a doesn't mind b hates c cleans d loves e doesn't like f doesn't mind g hates h doesn't have i loves j likes

5.3
1 Photo 1 shows the islands. Photo 2 shows a giant tortoise. Photo 3 shows sea turtles on sand.
2 a You can snorkel, kayak, or swim.
  b No, you don't. There are many ways to explore them.
  c No, they don't. They live on land, in the forests.
  d Penguins, turtles, flamingoes, sea lions, tortoises.
3 Katy: visiting museums, sightseeing, eating out
  Sara: snorkeling, camping, kayaking
  Tom: sunbathing, reading novels, swimming
4 reading novels, sightseeing, kayaking, snorkeling, sunbathing, swimming, taking a class, shopping

5.4
1 taking, watering, open, let, feed, give, check, take, pick, put, close, wash
2 a She's living in Bath.
  b He likes sleeping under a tree (all day).
  c She doesn't get any money. / None.
3 a ✓/✓/✗ b ✓/✓/✗ c ✗/✓/✗ d ✓/✗/✓
4 a Open / them / night b her c don't / dishes / them d him e it

5.5
1 a safe b cheap c messy d boring e near
2 a F b T c T d F
3 1 d 2 c 3 a 4 b

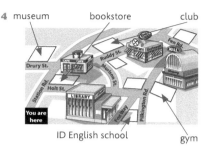

4 museum bookstore club
  ID English school gym

61

Phrase Bank

This Phrase Bank is organized by topics.

Greetings
Unit 1
Nice / Good to meet / see you.
Hello! Nice / Good to meet / see you, too.
How are you (doing)?
How's it going?
What's up?
Fine, thanks.
I'm well, thank you.
Good, thanks.
Things are good / not so good. Not bad.
What about you? / And you?
What's new?
Not much.
Bye for now.
See you later.

Personal information
Unit 1
Are you Peruvian?
Yes, I am. / No, I'm not.
What's your (first) name?
Hi! My name's Maria.
How do you spell your last name / that?
Do you have any brothers and sisters?
I have five brothers and sisters.
What nationality are you?
I'm American. I'm 18 (years old).
I'm 21 (today).
I'm from New York.
Is your mother British?
Yes, she is. / No, she isn't. She's Canadian.
What's your address / phone number / email (address)?
My address is 85 Brown Street.
Where are you from?

Unit 2
How old are you?
Where do you live?
In Madrid, because I work there.
What's your full name?
Do you have a pet?

Your opinion
Unit 1
I think Malala is a very intelligent person.
Yuck! This coffee is horrible.
It's a very cool city.
It's an amazing place.
Yes, I agree.
I think she's ridiculous.
I disagree.

Unit 5
Do you like camping?
I prefer yoga because I enjoy relaxing.
I don't agree. For me ...
I don't like watching TV.
I don't either.
What do you like doing on vacation?
I really like walking.
What about shopping?
We both love it.
In my opinion that's a cheap, fun vacation.
It's an OK place to live.
The most interesting place is probably the racetrack.
I don't mind doing the dishes.
I hate doing the laundry.
I love cell phones, but sometimes ring tones are annoying.

Routine
Unit 2
Do you exercise regularly?
Yes, I do. / No, I don't.
Do you often go to bed late?
How many hours do you sleep?
On average, around seven hours a night.
How often do you go to a café?
Every day after work.
I always have a shower at night before bed.
What time do you get up during the week?
I get up at about six thirty in the morning.
I go to school at seven o'clock from Monday to Friday.
I go to the gym for an hour before / after school.
I have an important meeting on Wednesday.
What do you do on weekends?
When do you go to the grocery store?

Family and relationships
Unit 2
Do you have a girlfriend?
Do you have any brothers or sisters?
No, I'm an only child.
Do you live with your parents?
No, I don't. I live with my girlfriend. / Yes, I do.
How many cousins do you have?
What's your father's name?
Where does your family live?

Phrase Bank

Telling the time
Unit 2
He wakes up at 8:00 a.m.
I go to school at six forty-five.
I usually get home at around six fifteen p.m.

Jobs
Unit 3
What do you do?
What's your job?
Where are you working?
I'm a …

Actions in progress
Unit 3
What are you doing (at the moment)?
I'm watching TV.
Nothing special.
Are you coming for coffee?
Where are you going?

Feelings
Unit 3
I'm not hungry.
I'm thirsty.

Offers
Unit 3
Do you want / Would you like a chocolate cookie?
No, thanks. I don't like them.
Do you want to watch TV?
Would you like a drink?
Yes, please. Black coffee, no sugar.
Would you like to go out?

On the phone
Unit 3
Hi. This is Maddie.
Are you busy?
Actually, yes, I'm cooking dinner.
Yes, I am. / Not really, I'm fine.
Can I call you later?
I can't hear you. Bye!
Meet you at the subway station? Let's go!
My battery's dying.
Nice talking to you.
No problem.
Sorry, wrong number.
Talk to you later.
The line's busy.

Weather and months
Unit 3
How's the weather in Chicago?
It's usually very rainy.
What's the temperature today?
It's about twenty-eight degrees.
What's the weather usually like there?
It's really hot and sunny.
What's your favorite month / season?
My birthday is in March.

Giving reasons
Unit 3
Why are you learning English?
Because I like it. / For pleasure.
For my job / school / college.
I have to pass an exam.
I need to write emails at work. / To communicate with people (face to face).
I want to travel / emigrate.
Why not?

Can
Unit 4
Can you run two kilometers?
I can, but not very well.
No, I can't. Not at all.
Yes, I can. Well, I think so.
I can speak two other languages.

Phrase Bank

Clothes

Unit 4
What's he wearing?
He's wearing black shorts and an old T-shirt.
Whose sweater is this? Is it yours?
No, it's not mine.
I have about twenty pairs of jeans.

Shopping

Unit 4
Can I help you?
Can I see those boots?
What color?
We have them in black or brown.
Black, please.
What size?
Can I try them on?
The fitting rooms are over there.
How much is it / are they?
Here's my credit card.
Please, enter your PIN number.
Here you are. / There you go.
Here's your receipt.
Have a nice day.

Sports

Unit 4
I don't / can't play baseball.
I go surfing every weekend.
My friends play soccer every weekend.
Our country is (usually) good at judo.

Directions

Unit 5
Are there any banks near here?
Do you know where the mall is?
Yes, go straight and turn right / left at the stoplight.
Is there a movie theater around here?
Yes, it's on Market Street.
Where's the bookstore?

Instructions

Unit 5
Don't forget to close the windows.
Please, feed my cat and my dog.
Remember to water the plants.

Other useful expressions

Unit 1
Are those / these your keys?
These are her keys.
This is my pen.
Can you say that again, please?
Don't worry about it.
Excuse me.
How do you spell ... / that?
I don't understand.
I'm online with my boyfriend.
Is that hotel in Spain?
Is that your bag?
Me, too.
Oh, sorry. / I'm sorry.
Sure ...
What are these in English?
They're windows.
It's a door.
This is my friend, Lucas.
What's the opposite of strong?
What are these?
What's that?
Yes, it is. / No, it isn't. It's in Mexico.
Yes, they are. / No, they aren't.
You're welcome.

Unit 2
What day is it today?
What do you usually do at Christmas?
Happy birthday!
Congratulations!
Enjoy your meal!
Happy New Year!
Have a good trip!
Merry Christmas!

Unit 3
Who's that?
What does she do?
She's a singer?

Unit 4
I love to go to salons.
I like to watch my team win.
My closet is small but clean and organized.

Word List

This is a reference list. To check pronunciation of any individual words, you can use a talking dictionary.

Unit 1

Countries
Argentina
Brazil
Canada
Chile
China
Ecuador
India
Japan
Korea
Peru
Portugal
Spain
The UK
The U.S.

Nationalities
American
Argentinian
Brazilian
British
Canadian
Chilean
Chinese
Ecuadorian
Indian
Korean
Peruvian
Portuguese
Spanish

Opinion adjectives
amazing
cool
excellent
fantastic
horrible
important
intelligent
interesting
OK
rich
ridiculous
terrible

Numbers 11-100
11 eleven
12 twelve
13 thirteen
14 fourteen
15 fifteen
16 sixteen
17 seventeen
18 eighteen
19 nineteen
20 twenty
21 twenty-one
22 twenty-two
23 twenty-three
30 thirty
31 thirty-one
32 thirty-two
40 forty
41 forty-one
50 fifty
60 sixty
70 seventy
80 eighty
90 ninety
100 one hundred

Personal objects
a backpack
earrings
glasses
keys
a laptop / computer
a lipstick
a pencil
a phone
a sandwich
an umbrella
a wallet

Colors
blue
black
brown
green
orange
pink
purple
red
yellow

Adjectives
big
cheap
expensive
good
new
old
real
small
strong
weak
young

Unit 2

Places
café
church
gym
grocery store
home
party
school
work

Days of the week
Monday
Tuesday
Wednesday
Thursday
Friday
Saturday
Sunday

Morning routine
brush my teeth
exercise
get dressed
get up
have breakfast
leave home
make the bed
shave
take a shower
wake up

Family members
aunt
boyfriend
brother
child(ren)
couple
cousin(s)
daughter
father
girlfriend
grandfather
grandmother
grandparent(s)
husband
mother
nephew
niece
parent(s)
partner
sibling(s)
sister
son
twin(s)
uncle
wife

Frequency adverbs
always
usually
often
sometimes
occasionally
never

Holidays
Carnival
Christmas
Day of the Dead
New Year ('s Eve)

Unit 3

Weather words
Nouns
cloud
fog
rain
snow
sun
wind

Adjectives
cloudy
foggy
rainy
snowy
sunny
windy

Temperature
cold
cool
hot
warm

Months
January
February
March
April
May
June
July
August
September
October
November
December

Seasons
fall
spring
summer
winter

Unit 4

Sports
baseball
basketball
bike riding (cycling)
football
golf
handball
hockey
martial arts
rugby
running
skateboarding
skiing
soccer
surfing
swimming
(table) tennis
volleyball

Professions
babysitter
journalist
secretary
teacher

Clothes items
belt
blouse
boots
dress
jacket
pants
sandals
shirt
shoes
shorts
skirt
sneakers
socks
suit
sweater
tie
T-shirt

Unit 5

Places around town
bar
bookstore
bridge
club
hotel
library
mall
movie theater
museum
park
racetrack
restaurant
river
stadium
swimming pool
theater

Word List

Vacation activities
buying souvenirs
camping
cooking
dancing
eating out
hiking
kayaking
reading novels
sightseeing
snorkeling
sunbathing
swimming
taking a class
visiting museums

House sitting
don't let the cat out
feed the cat / dog
give the cat some water
open / close the windows
pick up / put the mail on the table
turn on / off the lights
walk the dog
water the plants

Adjectives
boring
cheap
dangerous
expensive
fun
messy
neat
safe

Richmond
58 St Aldates
Oxford
OX1 1ST
United Kingdom

ISBN: 978-84-668-3250-2
Sixth Reprint: 2024
CP: 105577

© Richmond / Santillana Global S.L. 2019

All rights reserved. No part of this book may be reproduced, stored in a retrieval system or transmitted in any form by any means, electronic, mechanical, photocopying, recording or otherwise, without the prior permission in writing of the Publisher.

Publishing Director: Deborah Tricker
Publisher: Luke Baxter
Media Publisher: Luke Baxter
Managing Editor: Laura Miranda
Content Developers: Paul Seligson, Deborah Goldblatt, Neil Wood
Editors: Sarah Curtis, Hilary McGlynn
Proofreaders: Lily Khambata, Diyan Leake, Rachael Williamson
Design Manager: Lorna Heaslip
Cover Design: Lorna Heaslip
Design & Layout: Rob Briggs (ROARR Design), Jon Fletcher Design
Photo Researcher: Magdalena Mayo
Audio Production: John Marshall Media Inc.

We would like to thank all those who have given their kind permission to reproduce material for this book:

SB Illustrators: Alexandra Barbarozza, Alexandre Matos, Beach-o-matic, Bernardo Franca, Bill Brown, Guillaume Gennet, Diego Loza, Gus Morais, Alvaro Nuñez, Klayton Luz, Leonardo Teixeira, Martins CG Studio, Rico

WB Illustrators: Alexandre Matos, Andrew Pagram, Vicente Mendonça

SB Photos:
V. Atmán; 123RF/Juan Bauitista Cofreces, Antonio Balaguer Soler, Tatjana Baibakova, oleksiy, Gerold Grotelueschen, ALFREDO COSENTINO, Julian Peters, Cathy Yeulet; ALAMYAKP Photos, Peter Forsberg/People, WENN Ltd, Pictorial Press Ltd, Simon Grosset, Ilene MacDonald, Collection Christophel, Stefan Sollfors, Inner Vision Pro, dennizn, Granger Historical Archive, Don Douglas, Michael Wheatley, Everett Collection Inc, Wm. Baker/GhostWorx, dcphoto, Martin Thomas Photography, carlos cardetas, AF Archive; GETTY IMAGES SALES SPAIN/Fuse, Enjoynz, FOX, E+, Anna Frajitova, Stockbyte, Amarita, AJ_Watt, Londoneye, tBoyan, Tomazl, Xavier Arnau, TriggerPhoto, CJ Rivera, Nikada, Maskot, Zxvisual, Lisafx, Caziopeia, Onston, Drbimages, Vostok, Klaus Vedfelt, wakila, Phive2015, Alvarez, AntonioGuillem, Andresr, Byrdyak, DimaChe, CSA Images, Eyewave, Gerenme, Kaantes, Jabiru, Klasu Tiedge, Stockcam, Ipopba, CaronB, Jeff Kravitz, Dragonimages, Bill Baptist, Win McNamee, Nazar_ab, Pingebat, Serts, Leeser87, JoKMedia, Pekic, Jaromila, Mr.nutnuchit Phutsawagung/EyeEm, NurPhoto, Bas Vermolen, Boston Globe, Erik Isakson, Image Source, Robynmac, Scanrail, Klaus Tiedge, Totororo, WPA Pool, Wsfurlan, PaoloGaetano, Adie Bush, Alan Graf, Ansonmiao, Ricky Vigil, bowdenimages, Chalabala, Cindy Ord, Designalldone, FatCamera, Heshphoto, LJM Photo, Luis Cataneda, Martin-dm, Mixdabass, Nancy Ney, Rafael Fabres, Polka Dot, Ridofranz, StockFood, Janoka82, Tuan Tran, Westend61, icarmen13, karandaev, Adam Gault, Ajr_images, Buyenlarge, Eric McCandless, Dreamnikon, Drewhadley, EnolaBrain, Eri Morita, FSTOPLIGHT, Grandriver, Hillwoman2, Maica, Gkrphoto, Flavijus, Kali9, Flashpop, Harold Stiver/EyeEm, Georgeclerk, Dmitry_7, JackF, Filadendron, Bettmann, Eva-Katalin, Don Farrall, Yvdavyd, Fudio, Futureimage, TangMan Photography, Hero Images, Ildo Frazao, Jay's Photo, Jesse Grant, Karinsasaki, Karwai Tang, Lovelypeace, Arnab Guha Photography, Rose_Carson, Ryan MacVay, Sam Edwards, Shapecharge, Simoningate, Svariophoto, The_burtons, Igor Kisselev - www.close-up.biz, 10'000 Hours, Photo by Ivan Dmitri/Michael Ochs Archives, BamBamImages, Tom Werner, spooh, Pixelfit, Recep-bg, Tom Merton, Gpointstudio, BraunS, RichLegg, Juice Images, Karin Dreyer, Karl Tapales, Kevin Winter, YinYang, Thinkstock, Ligia Botero, Michael Tran, Mike Cameron, Momentimages, Morsa Images, Oneinchpunch, Brian Cullen/EyeEm, PeopleImages, Raymond Hall, Rustemgurler, South_agency, Stocksnapper, Tim Robberts, Travis Payne, Theo Wargo, Spinkle, Ayzek, AlasdairJames, Andersen Ross, Ariel Skelley, Carsten Koall, Dan Bannister, Thatpichai, Gabriel Bouys, Inti St Clair, Istanbulimage, Jamie Garbutt, Johner Images, Joseph Okpako, Jupiterimages, Ryan McVay, Merinka, Mikkelwilliam, Mitchell Funk, Mlsfotografia, Pacific Press, Paul Bradbury, Peathegee Inc, Peter Cade, Samir Hussein, Serhil Brovko, Stephen Marks, Steve Granitz, Ullstein Bild, _human/iStock, Anadolu Agency, OJO images, Marcaux, Caracterdesign, David De Lossy, Digital Vision, Dzphotogallery, FS Productions, Image_By_Kenny, Kryssia Campos, LauriPatterson, Martin Barraud, Shannon Finney, SinghaphanAllB, Zero Creatives, franckreporter, Axel Bernstorff, Aonip, Fabrice LEROUGE, JGI/Jamie Grill, Lutsina Tatiana, MakiEni's Photo, Mario Gutierrez, Michael Dunning, Philippe Regard, Philippe TURPIN, Piotr Pawelczyk, Adam Lunde/EyeEm, Aurelien Maunier, Crady Von Pawlak, Education Images, Kansas City Star, MangoStar_Studio, Asia Images Group, Mike Prior, Alexander Tamargo, Abel Halasz/EyeEm, MiguelMalo, Lawcain, Yulia_Davidovich, C Squared Studios, ColorBlind Images, ElenaNichizhenova, Jonathan Paciullo, Malcolm P Chapman, Maya Karkalicheva, PeterHermesFurian, Vi Ngoc Minh Khue, AleksandarGeorgiev, Richard E. Aaron, Buena Vista Images, Enrique Diaz/7cero, Jason Merritt/TERM, Jonas Hafner/EyeEm, Julie Moquet/EyeEm, Katra Toplak/EyeEm, Larry Busacca/PW18, Oksana Vejus/EyeEm, PamelaJoeMcFarlane, Razvan Chisu/EyeEm, Tim Clayton-Corbis, Burcu Atalay Tankut, Dan Thornberg/EyeEm, Dave and Les Jacobs, Elizabeth Fernandez, Lars Baron, Quynh Anh Nguyen, Teresa Recena/EyeEm, The Washington Post, Axelle/Bauer-Griffin, Classen Rafael/EyeEm, Color Day Production, Fabiano Santos/EyeEm, Jose Luis Pelaez Inc, Monkeybusinessimages, Nils Hendrik Mueller, Santiago Bluguermann, Aaron Fortunato/EyeEm, Andriy Mykhalchevskyy, Sara Herrlander/EyeEm, Science Photo Library, Peter Macdiarmid, Athletea Widjaja/EyeEm, Cynthia Lafrance/EyeEm, Hinterhaus Productions, James Haliburton/EyeEm, Gallo Images-Stuart Fox, chokkicx/Digital Vision, Benedetta Barbanti/EyeEm, Caiaimage/Agnieszka Olek, Szabo Ervin-Edward/EyeEm, Jules Frazier Photography, Thomas Roetting/LOOK-foto, Paul Mansfield Photography, De Agostini Picture Library, Jon Feingersh Photography Inc, John Fenigersh Photography Inc, JB Lacroix, LIU JIN, Michael Rheault - madfire@gmail.com, Compassionate Eye Foundation/Gary Burchell, Poba, ANDREYGUDKOV; ISTOCKPHOTO/Getty Images Sales Spain, Susan Chiang, Juanmonino, Chmiel; NASA; SHUTTERSTOCK/Arts Illustrated Studios, Moviestore Collection, ESB Professional, Swan Gallet/WWD, MarianVejcik, Happy Together, Ken McKay, AlexLMX; Louisville Convention & Visitor Bureau; Tumbleweed Tiny House Company; Kaitlyn Schlicht; Kelly Bruno; Dotta; Helen Chelton López de Haro; Jorge Cueto; United Nations; ARCHIVO SANTILLANA

WB Photos:
J. Jaime; 123RF/Fabrizio Troiani, brulove, Tatiana Popova; ALAMY/Steve Skjold, Michey, Skyscan Photolibrary, Image Source Plus, Erwin Zueger, Dmitry Melnikov, AF Archive, Elena Elisseeva, Zoonar GmbH, F1online digitale Bildagentur GmbH; GETTY IMAGES SALES SPAIN/RB, Liam Norris, SolStock, JoKMedia, Paul Bradbury, By Vesi_127, Floortje, Kupicoo, Steve Granitz, Hackisan, Hero Images, Nattrass, Thomas Francois, Antonello, Drbimages, Electravk, NetaDegany, DigiStu, D-Keine, Photoservice, Gofotograf, Subjug, David Lees, MarianKoplo, Rob Kroenert, Gradyreese, Karaandaev, Kojihirano, G-stockstudio, NicoElNino, Thinkstock, Zak Kendal, Altayb, Donvictorio, Georgeclerk, Guenterguni, Jeff Greenberg, John Rowley, JohnnyGreig, Kevin Mazur, David Livingston, OksanaKiian, Philipphoto, Roger Kisby, Sam Edwards, Taylor Hill, Xavierarnau, 10'000 Hours, Morsa Images, Kevin Mazur/Billboard Awards 2014, Chris Ryan, Westend61, Image Source, IakovKalinin, Phil Fisk, Diana Miller, Ismailciydem, Kali9, Liesel Bockl, MachineHeadz, Deepblue4you, Mike Kemp, Noel Vasquez, PeopleImages, Dcdr, David Buchan, Sezeryadigar, South_agency, Tim Robberts, Caroline Sale, Chris Clinton, Fiona Goodall, Dave J Hogan, James Devaney, Jamie Garbutt, Jeffrey Mayer, Johner Images, Jupiterimages, Michael Kovac, Oliver Furrer, Istetiana, China Photos, Terry O'Neill, Yasser Chalid, Anthony Harvey, Cecilie_Arcurs, Hulton Archive, Ida Mae Astute, Axelle/Bauer-Griffin, LauriPatterson, Marc Romanelli, Martin Hospach, Newstockimages, JGI/Jamie Grill, Photos.com Plus, Stefanie Grewel, Victor Ovies Arenas, Andrew Merry, Jay L. Clendenin, Jeffrey Richards, Gareth Cattermole, Gonzalo Marroquin, Jonathan Paciullo, Oktay Ortakcioglu, RightFieldStudios, Robyn Breen Shinn, istock/Thinkstock, Stanton J Stephens, DEA / G. NIMATALLAH, Dave and Les Jacobs, Rajibul Hasan/EyeEm, Teresa Recena/EyeEm, Ian Gavan, Imv, BJI/Blue Jean Images, Caiaimage/Tom Merton, Gints Ivuskans/EyeEm, Jose Luis Pelaez Inc, Monkeybusinessimages, Tim Clayton - Corbis, Caiaimage/Sam Edwards, Dan Thornberg / EyeEm, Mendowong Photography, Science Photo Library, Tatiana Dyuvbanova/EyeEm, Jules Frazier Photography, Universal History Archive, Dennis Fischer Photography, Simpson33, Julia Finney; ISTOCKPHOTO/Getty Images Sales Spain; SHUTTERSTOCK/Kseniia Perminova, threerocksimages, Sergey Peterman, Ilya Sviridenko, PhotoHouse, eurobanks, AJR_photo, hxdbxxy, kurhan; ARCHIVO SANTILLANA

The Publisher has made every effort to trace the owner of copyright material; however, the Publisher will correct any involuntary omission at the earliest opportunity.

Printed in Brazil by Forma Certa Gráfica Digital
Lote: 800.392